Who Am I ...

Now That I'm Not
Who I Was?

also by Connie Goldman

Tending the Earth, Mending the Spirit
The Healing Gifts of Gardening
(with Richard Mahler)

The Ageless Spirit
Reflections on Living Life to the Fullest in Midlife and the Years Beyond

The Gifts of Caregiving
Stories of Hardship, Hope and Healing

Late Life Love
Romance and New Relationships in Later Years

Secrets of Becoming a Late Bloomer
Staying Creative, Aware and Involved in Mid-Life and Beyond
(with Richard Mahler)

Who Am I ...

Now That I'm Not Who I Was?

Conversations with Women
in Midlife and Beyond

Connie Goldman

NODIN PRESS

ISBN: 978-1-932472-92-9

Library of Congress Cataloging-in-Publication Data

Goldman, Connie.
Who am I-- : now that I'm not who I was? : conversations with women in mid-life and beyond / by Connie Goldman.
    p. cm.
ISBN 978-1-932472-92-9
1. Middle-aged women. 2. Middle-aged women--Psychology.
3. Older women--Psychology. I. Title.
  HQ1059.4.G69 2009
  305.244--dc22
                                    2009031121

Cover photos, clockwise from upper left: digitalskillet (istock), JJRD (istock), Cliff Parnell (istock), Sheryl Yazolino Griffin (istock), Michael Svoboda (dreamstime).

design and layout: John Toren

Nodin Press, LLC
530 N. Third Street,
Suite 120
Minneapolis, MN
55401

To all women –
there are life lessons to be learned
from others as well as from inside
your very self.
Listen, look and learn.

Acknowledgments

All of my writing over the years has been based on telling other peoples stories. At this time I'm going to tell one of my own. It's the story of how this book came into being.

For the past three years at the annual national conference of the American Society on Aging, I've been participating in a session called, *On Being An Older Woman: A Conversation.* And indeed it was a conversation where the women who attended our discussion group did most of the talking. With honesty and openness each woman shared her thoughts and experiences related to her aging; fears and losses, accomplishments and growth, doubts and disappointments, losses and learning. There were hugs of support, understanding and tears, laughter and acceptance.

In the midst of our session during the third year, as I sat deeply involved with the stories, I suddenly made the connection between those stories and the book I had been writing during the previous year—the book you hold in your hand. This is why I'm expressing my gratitude to Martha Holstein, Joan Ditzion, and Phyllis Mitzen for continuing to hold their annual sharing sessions and making a space for women to learn about themselves through the stories of others.

Of course I owe thanks to my publisher, Norton Stillman, and my talented and supportive editor and layout designer, John Toren. A thank you also to Lane Stiles at Fairview Press who shared his thoughts and expertise with me in the early stages of this book. Certainly I owe my deep appreciation as well to all of the women who generously allowed me to tell their stories in this book.

Writing a book can be an isolated activity. I'm fortunate that I share an office with my lover, companion and life partner Ken Tilsen. Every time I said, "I need someone to read this chapter and tell me if it works," he picked up his red pencil and helped me through my crisis. I can't write THANK YOU enough times for his astute comments and generous help.

– Connie Goldman

Contents

Introduction

"The old woman I shall become will be quite different from the woman I am now. Another "I" is beginning."

— George Sand

Although I can't credit the authors because I lost the original sources long ago, I often quote the following phrases. *"Age has given me what I was looking for my entire life; it gave me, me!"* and *"The journey in between who you once were and who you are now becoming is where the dance of life really takes place."*

I consider the quotes above to resonate truth. Yet there are other phrases, implications, and innuendoes in American advertising, marketing, and conversation that perpetrate a different image of aging. The truth is that we live in a world where a great deal of individual energy is often expended working to avoid, delay, or mask the changes that accompany the aging process. Americans have an appetite for staying young, almost an insatiable hunger to remain unwrinkled, thin, and youthful. Millions surgically alter their appearance, or struggle in some way to resist, delay, deny, outwit, or camouflage the dreaded enemy—aging.

As I write this, I have on my desk four of many magazines I've collected that carry such messages. Their covers headline the story inside. "The New Pill That Can End Aging," "The Quest to Beat Aging," "The New Cure for Aging," and "Sixty is the New Thirty."

I'm well aware that other messages are also being broadcast widely by the media—messages that encourage people in mid-life and the years beyond to eat well, exercise regularly, and keep their minds active. I totally embrace this positive thread of encouragement and advice, and all programs directed toward keeping our minds and bodies functioning as well as they can. As for me, at age 78, I strive to exercise five days a week, cut down on excesses in eating, and keep my mind alert.....while also forgiving those inevitable memory lapses.

However, when I write and speak about reclaiming aging, I'm referring to an aspect of aging that I believe isn't getting the attention it deserves. There are changes and challenges that come into each of our individual lives that offer us the experience, not just to grow old but to grow whole; to explore who we are now that we're not who we were. Several writers have attempted to describe what this exploration of ourselves is all about. Here are the words of only a few.

"The task of the midlife transition is to make peace with the past and prepare for the future....midlife brings with it an invitation to accept ourselves as we truly are."

– Paula Payne Hardin

"In the second half of life, our old compasses no longer work. The magnetic fields alter. The new compass that we need cannot be held in our hand, only in our hearts. We read it not with our mind alone, but with our soul. Now we yearn for wholeness."

– Mark Gerzon

I want to tell people approaching and perhaps fearing age that it is a time of discovery. If they say, 'Of what?' I can only answer, 'We must each find out for ourselves, otherwise it won't be a discovery. I want to say ....if at the end of your life you have only yourself, it is much. Look, and you will find."

– Florida Scott Maxwell

During the 30 years I've been producing public radio programs, writing and speaking on subjects related to aging, I've often quoted the poet Muriel Rukyhauser, who said, "The world isn't made of atoms, it's made of stories." I believe we have the possibility of learning about ourselves from the stories of others. Hearing or reading the story of someone you don't know and may never meet can awaken some personal truth or wisdom inside of you.

For this book I've collected conversations with 18 women between the ages of 50 and 80. Each tells of her own life experiences, challenges and learning, sharing her personal truth in her own words. I believe they've revealed themselves honestly and openly in an act of verbal undress. Their stories are about the passion and possibilities of change in their lives throughout the years, about learning and growth, about discovery and wisdom.

These stories are not exceptional or rare. When people ask me how I found such interesting, thoughtful, and talkative people, I smile and tell them the truth. There are millions of such stories out there, everyone has a story of many chapters, everyone! As we age and grow we write our own stories by living them. Each person, including you, makes choices, decisions, take actions, and makes plans. Everyone has the potential of growth, change, learning, and growing.

Not every story in this collection will speak directly to you, yet you may be surprised when a paragraph or two touches a personal awareness and offers you insight, comfort, and confirmation that aging can mean something other than fear, decline, and loss. I've added some brief comments labeled *Afterthoughts* at the end of each conversation in the hope that they might also offer you food for thought.

I'm convinced that the challenge of aging isn't to stay young; it's not only to grow old but to grow whole—to come into your own. The aging process is woven into human destiny. It's your time to embrace that challenge and figure out who you are now that you're not who you were.

Vicki (age 63)

I am seeking, I am striving, I am in it with all my heart.

— Vincent Van Gogh

Vicki was eager to talk with me the day of our appointment. We took off our coats, sat down in a booth, ordered our coffee and she immediately began talking.

The title of your book really has an interesting twist. Now, at the age of 63, I think I've discovered who I really am … now that I'm not who I was. I feel that I've discovered things about myself that have brought me to a place of knowing and understanding.

I built my life and my career on the rules and values I was exposed to as I was growing up. One thing I learned early on was that you are what you do. I remember in high school I tried to figure out who I was. I wasn't the most popular or the homecoming queen or a cheerleader; I didn't have an identity. I spent my time trying to figure out where I could fit in and get respect and acceptance.

When I went to college I found an identity and place to fit in. It was during the Vietnam war, a radical time, and I was on an unusually radical campus. My feelings and opinions about how I felt about my country, what was right and wrong with that war, became my identity.

Fresh out of college I was offered a job at a large company where I had interned during the summer. My first day at work I was handed a sheet of paper describing my job—my identity was now defined by the words on that page. This is your title, this is our dress code, and these are your duties and responsibilities. At this company, this is who you are.

It wasn't long before I got married to my long-time boyfriend. My husband got a job in a different city so I left my job and we moved. My last job description impressed my future employer. I became the new head of marketing and advertising for a large company. Was I qualified for that job? Absolutely not. Was I lucky to be at the right place at the right time? Yes, I sure was. Once again I had that job description that defined who I was. One of the clients I was assigned to work with was a television network. I quickly learned that 'the network' became my 'net worth.' The most important thing I learned on that job was that who you know can help you move up in the business world.

When the company I was working for went through a transition and a new CEO took charge, I suddenly became an inherited employee and not someone he had chosen. I stayed on for a couple of years until the television network connections I had made paid off. I got a phone call from the head of the television network saying, "We have a job for you". That call defined who I was going to be next.

So I was off to New York. I had a great job and I loved my work. My job was to convince the advertisers and affiliate stations how much better our television network was than the competitors. As so often happens in the corporate world, there came a time when a new management took over. He who buys the company brings in their own people and makes their own rules. I lost my job and began wondering what I was going to do next. Nothing defined me anymore. I had lost my professional identity.

The work I had been doing is what I knew and what I had to offer. I got the idea to set up my own business, make a proposal to the network I had just left and continued doing promotion for several of the departments and television shows I had worked with previously. I set up my own business at a time when I couldn't even spell entrepreneur! After my first year in business my accountant told me that I'd better land a major account because I had used up all my personal contacts. I asked him for advice and direction and he said, "I think the aging market is coming; it's going to be a big field. Not a lot of people understand, it's waiting for you, Vicki." That became my new identity.

I set up my own business at a time when I couldn't even spell entrepreneur!

For the next 17 years I pursued clients that had a product or service for a growing senior market. I started out by getting clients in the investment business. I co-authored a book entitled *Banking on the Mature Market*. Ironically, that book gave me and my co-author the unexpected opportunity to become recognized as leading authorities on the mature market. Besides banking I had an interest in television left over from my previous position. I produced, packaged, and marketed a series of exercise videos with The Dancing Grannies. I felt I had established myself when mail arrived simply addressed to The Dancing Grannies and the mail delivery person left it in my mailbox without a street address on the envelope.

The next change on my horizon dawned when I was in my

50's. The world of account executives had changed and I was giving my sales pitch on selling an aging market to young women in their 20's and early 30's. I believe they listened politely to my pitch but didn't absorb a word. It didn't mean anything to them. In spite of the fact that their client was a large insurance company seeking to market to persons in their 50' and 60's, those handling the account were not open to my message. I think that appointment was when I started to deeply resent the hoops I had to jump through to get a new client. It was starting to be a pain in the neck to pitch and call, follow up and call, keep asking when they were going to sign the contract, all of it. The whole routine became more and more frustrating, laborious and aggravating for me.

One Friday morning I woke up and my ankles were very swollen. By the end of that weekend, both of my legs were so swollen that I couldn't put on any of my slacks. I couldn't put on shoes either. When my husband drove me to the doctor I couldn't sit up in the car. I had to slide into the back seat and lay down because I couldn't bend my knees. My doctor sent me to a kidney specialist and I was diagnosed with nephritis. For many months I couldn't wear my regular clothes or put shoes on my swollen feet. I couldn't work at all for many months, almost a year.

I was still trying to maintain my business but I didn't want to be seen. The medication I was on made my face swollen and puffy and I felt that my body too was bloated and grotesque. Looking and feeling like that, I couldn't make appointments to meet with people. It was a horrible time for me. I wasn't sure my life would ever be normal again.

It was at that point that I really began to appreciate the value of good health. By the time I had fully recovered a year later, my priorities had changed. Thankfully, I've not had a reoccurrence. I don't know whether I'm in remission or if in the future I'll have a reoccurrence of the disease. I live with uncertainty yet with new awareness.

I'm able to look at my life now with a different and new perspective. One of the most important things I had learned was that I could live on far less money than I thought. This realization made it easier for me to stop pursuing contracts I didn't enjoy.

I guess we never know what might come along in our lives next. One day my husband told me he had volunteered to help build a home in our area for an Iraq veteran who had lost and arm and a leg. It was for an organization called *Homes For Our Troups*. I remember thinking I'd go along with him to his first appointment with that group just to see what that project was about. The organization was dedicated to building homes for severely injured veterans and their families at no cost to them. The project was just getting started at that time but they hoped to expand throughout the entire country. The plan was for the cost of everything needed for building the homes to be covered by contributions, foundation grants, and fund raisers, but that plan wasn't in place yet. They had a strong start with an anonymous donation of ten million dollars. I was very impressed and very touched as well. I could see that this project was vitally important for soldiers who had been wounded and disabled in the Iraq and Afghanistan wars, and also had great potential for pulling in sponsors.

One of the most important things I had learned was that I could live on far less money than I thought.

I offered to volunteer and approached the credit union where I had found my first job, as it too had started as a grass roots organization. I had a strong feeling that these two groups should get together. I brought in the credit unions as the first sponsor for the project. I did it as a volunteer because I believed in what they were doing. The fallout from that success brought me the work I'm now doing. After some months I got a phone call from the founder of the group asking me if I knew of a public relations and marketing agency that they could employ to seek sponsors and grants and get the group and their work some press coverage.

I took the job, renewed in my enthusiasm because of the nature of the work. I witnessed an abundance

I no longer have that old urge to climb the professional ladder. I'm content with the meaningful work I'm doing.

of heartache because I was working very closely with each family. I learned very quickly that when a soldier is wounded, the entire family is wounded. It was extremely rewarding to meet with newspaper reporters or magazine writers who had a sincere interest in the story. I no longer had to pitch like the old days—now media was coming after me. I love this job, truly love it.

The organization has now built 40 homes around the country. This year they estimate they'll be able to build an equal number. I've been impressed by the generous contributions of the general contractors. They often donate materials and give extra time, talent, and sweat in spite of the fact that their businesses aren't as robust as they were before the housing bubble burst. There are many community supported events along the way, including a three-day building brigade and a volunteer day when neighbors and friends put the sod and lawn in and raise the flag on the newly constructed flag pole. It's a touching ceremony when the keys to the home are presented to the vet and his family.

Now that I'm in my 60's, I think I've reached a certain level of maturity and I no longer have that old urge to climb the professional ladder. I'm content with the meaningful work I'm doing. I used to struggle for that prestige to be a somebody. That was so important to me in my other jobs when I was younger. I needed peer group accolades from the boss and from my co-workers. This time around I have no ego involved. I want to help this organization because I see what good it does and what potential it has to grow and serve even more families of veterans. I've moved up in importance in the organization and I don't need the praise. There's a comfort in that. I feel like I've gotten out of my own way. The visibility I seek now isn't for me, it's for the cause. I see now, first hand, what war does to the family and I'm so happy to be associated with a cause that's helping these families rebuild their lives and move into a comfortable and secure home without having the burden of a mortgage.

Even when the waters are calm, I guess there's always the next challenge in life. It became obvious that Vicki's mother could no longer care for the large house on the farm in the Midwest where Vicki had grown up. The location was rather isolated, especially in winter, and her widowed mother lived there alone. Vicki had been making more frequent trips for visits. On one visit she asked her mother to come back with her to make the winter easier for both of them. Eventually the farm was sold and the move into her daughter's home became permanent.

After she first came to live with us she talked about being sad at leaving the farm. Mom had lived all of her married life there and I understood the grieving for her old life. I took her back to spend the summer with her old friends. We made a few trips back to the Midwest so she could remain reconnected with her past, see her friends. After her summer visits there I'd pick her up in early fall and take her back to live with us. After several of those trips I told Mom that I wasn't going to travel back and forth any more and that if she wanted to live with us she had to make a total commitment to move. I was relieved when Mom made the decision to make our home her home.

Mom moved in with us ten years ago—she's 87 now. At first it was hard, especially in the kitchen. Before we remodeled and enlarged our kitchen we were constantly in each other's way. Mom was always telling me how to make things, how I should do things as I prepared a meal, and it was driving me nuts! I felt I couldn't say things I wanted to say like, "Don't tell me how to do things, this is my kitchen." My husband was upset with all the wrangling going on, and things were going in a dangerous direction. We began to discuss remodeling the room and came up with a plan that gave us twice as much working space. Mom now has a whole corner, an entire space of her own to work in. One day I asked Mom to make the salad and when I came over to her space and told her to cut the radishes in smaller pieces she said, "I'm the boss in this space." We laughed. The conflicts in the kitchen are over.

There were many other things to sort, sift through and work out when Mom moved in. We didn't hesitate to talk honestly, share our needs and priorities, and deal with areas of potential conflict. I think it's wise to do this early on when someone is going to permanently share your space.

In time our friends became her friends and that made her adjustment easier. She hadn't as yet integrated into the greater community, although she was active and reasonably healthy. She gardened and cooked and did things around the house. At a certain point I suggested she venture out, make her own friends, and expand her activities. I was so proud of mom that she independently went to our local senior center, began participating in the activities, made new friends and now has gone to the yoga classes there for several years. She goes to theater with her new friends, and she's now taking computer classes. It's been an inspiration and a joy to have her with us these ten years. She's truly a remarkable woman.

I was so proud of mom that she independently went to our local senior center, began participating in the activities, made new friends and now has gone to the yoga classes there for several years.

Mom has a positive attitude, and as I look back I realized she raised me that way as well. I think that my attitude is part of everything coming together in my life at this time. I don't know what the remainder of my journey is but I know I'm more ready to deal with my aging. I don't have quite the stamina in the gym than I used to have, the arches of my feet hurt, the prescription for my glasses has gotten stronger, and there are many physical changes that are slowly happening. In spite of these changes I'm happy with a new understanding of what really makes me happy, and I sure am liking the journey of getting smarter about things. I feel blessed to have good friends, a supportive and loving husband, and a mom who's healthy, curious, and willing to learn at age 87.

I won't have a daughter to move in with later in my life, but I don't miss not having children. My husband and I made a conscious decision early in our marriage not to have children and I really never regretted it. I enjoy my friends grown children now but I never had any desire to have babies or raise young children.

When I was younger I never could have had a thought what I'm going to tell you now. When I'm 65 I'm going to have a birthday celebration like a friend of mine did a while ago. She called it her Medicare-Social Security birthday bash. It's a good time in my life now and I expect it to be then as well. I'm really blessed. I don't think my life could be any better. I really like who I am and where I'm at.

Working with the veterans has deepened my empathy and compassion. My problems are minor, theirs have changed everything in their lives. Giving back is now much more important to me than getting rich. As long as my husband and I have our health, have enough money to live comfortably and to pay our mortgage, we have everything we need.

My income has gone down considerably but somehow it doesn't matter to me. I've spent too much time and money shopping and accumulating stuff. I care so little about material things these days and that's an enormous change in my life. I actually think differently. I needed a new car a few months ago. In the past I always had to have a marquee car. This time I got a medium-priced, modest car and it drives just fine.

I can close my eyes at night and sleep without worrying about contracts being signing or presentations I have to give to clients, or make plans for airplanes I have to catch. I've learned a lot, it's been very humbling, and I have the satisfying feeling that what I'm doing is making a difference. I believe I'm in the best time of my life I feel centered, anchored, without stress, I'm at peace, I know who I am.

Things do not change, we change.

– Henry David Thoreau

AFTERTHOUGHTS

One of the reasons I chose to include Vicki's story in this collection of conversations with women is that the pattern of her work life might offer some insights into how our careers sometimes shape us, as opposed to us shaping them. Certainly not all of us have had positions as glamorous as Vicki's, yet circumstances in our work lives that give us a desired identity often influence our choice of career.

Vicki's illness and forced withdrawal from the work world resulted in dramatic changes for her. These days, downsizing, layoffs, and reorganization of businesses and workplaces may have the same effect for many others. Such events are financially disorienting and sometimes dangerous, but they also present opportunities for some of us to reconsider how we really want to live, and what occupation really brings us satisfaction. Pulling back, taking a break, a respite from the pattern of our work or routine, either voluntary or forced upon us, might provide a transition time that ultimately gives us a new perspective and a new direction.

Maybe even a brief respite—just a day sitting under a tree, a long walk in woods or just sitting in front of the fireplace and doing nothing—might open a time of reflection and change.

Mildred (age 73)

She is not rich that possesses much,
but she that is content with what she has

— Anonymous

I was immediately attracted to Mildred because of her warm, welcoming smile. We met in 3 feet of water in the swimming pool at the local Y. Later, in the dressing room, we had our first conversation. She didn't hesitate to express her philosophy. "I've experienced a lot as the years piled up, life has been my teacher," she told me almost as soon as our conversation began. Mildred hasn't traveled widely or delved into psychology or philosophy. She has lived what some would label 'an ordinary life.' Yet she has thought deeply in her own way, and during the conversations we've had since that first encounter in the pool, she has shared many insights with me. Mildred isn't one to give advice to others, but well she could. Here are some of her thoughts and reflections.

I had a hysterectomy after my fourth child and I've had two separate mastectomies. I have no females parts left. I decided to do the radical because I made the choice not to do the radiation. At the time drugs for cancer were new. I was told that I couldn't take any of them because I was quite young then. To avoid radiation I decided to have the mastectomies.

I'm flat-chested now but I'm comfortable with the way I look. If it makes others uncomfortable, it's their problem. What's more important to me than how I look on the outside is how I feel on the inside. I feel good. I'm here, I'm healthy. I'm not interested in wearing anything that looks like breasts or having those parts of my body rebuilt as some people do. The image I project to the world doesn't depend on my body. I hope others see me as more than a body. After all, a body is just a vessel to hold the soul, the whole of who I am. Maybe I look at mastectomy differently than some other women. My breasts were a diseased part of my body and I chose to get rid of them. For me it was a positive thing, not a negative. I guess I've had an easier time adjusting than some women who have had mastectomies.

All of that was several years ago and so far I'm cancer free. But I'm always aware that the cancer could return in some other part of my body. I have painful backaches that flair up unexpectedly. I guess I'm worried they might be cancer-related. But once I get the pain under control they no longer concern me much. I had a kidney problem a while ago and I was relieved and thankful to find that it wasn't cancer. I've learned over time to just live with these things. I've accepted the possibility that the cancer might return and I've chosen not to live in fear. I can't control some circumstances but I can control my reaction to them.

I'm enjoying where I'm at in my life at this time and I embrace who I am now. I laugh a lot and I try to remember to smile. I enjoy talking with friends and people I meet. Sometimes, when I look at folks I can tell how unhappy they are. I guess what I'd like to tell them is that their lives might be different if they could look at their lives like their glass is half full instead of half empty.

I'm happier at this stage of my life than ever before. I have a new kind of freedom. I'm finally feel free to do as I please and that's the good part of growing older. I also have less fear of death than of facing a difficult, painful dying process. What some people have to go through when they die is so difficult and painful for them and their families. I have no control over that event so I'm not going to spend time worrying about it. These days of my life are good. Sure things aren't perfect but in general things are good for me. I've learned as I've gone through life that keeping a positive attitude keeps my life on course.

I've learned as I've gone through life that keeping a positive attitude keeps my life on course.

I'm 73. But that's not old, you know. Oh yes, I know I'm in what's labeled "the later years" and I accept my age comfortably. Sometimes I hear myself saying that I'm 73 years young. I don't really like that expression. I guess it just slips out because I hear other people talk like that. But I'm not young and I sure wouldn't want to be young again. It doesn't make sense for older people to talk about staying young or living their later years trying to act young. I sure don't want to do that.

My married life has been mainly home centered. I was a mother, a wife, and a homemaker. I didn't work outside my home when I was married. We only had my husband's income, and as we had more children money became tight. I didn't want to work outside of my home but we needed the income. I've always been good at making clothes, so I began sewing wedding dresses and other apparel for customers. After a while I discovered that there was more money to be made in alterations. That gave me some extra income and it helped an awful lot.

When my dad died just about ten years ago he left me some money. That covered the things I wanted to buy or do for myself. I don't need to work at all any more. Social Security comes every month and I get a few stock dividends once in a while. It's no great amount of money but it's all I need.

Three years ago I fell down two steps. Actually, that was the worst physical problem I ever had to deal with. The result of that fall was a leg broken in three places. I was out of town when it happened and I ended up in the hospital. My experience there was really terrible. I had to have help to go to the bathroom but a nurse didn't come when I put my call light on. I had to manage myself and I fell. My care in that hospital was very poor and I don't think the treatment for the three breaks was handled well. They never healed right. My foot is about 15 degrees off and I'll never walk correctly, but I'm thankful I can walk. I guess I see my glass half full. I think I've learned to look at my life that way.

Some things have been harder for me to deal with than my physical health. I've lost two grandsons. One was only eight months old. He died in his crib. It was SIDS, Sudden Infant Death Syndrome. The other death was a 27-year-old grandson. He was a difficult child; very bright, very manipulative. His father was immature and his mother, my daughter, was inconsistent and permissive. She would often bring him over and just leave him with me for several days. I never knew when she would come back to get him. I really was one of the adults that raised him. I just couldn't let that child be left alone. If she left him with her husband, his father, he would take him to the bar with him, and to other places that weren't appropriate for a young child. I felt I had to take care of him. As my grandson grew older he had lots of trouble with drugs. He tried to give up the addiction but couldn't. Because he was dealing drugs he served a couple of prison terms. My husband and I would visit him in prison but nobody else in the family did. He was a hurting person. It's no wonder that his life turned out as it did.

I don't choose to go into the details of his death with you but I can tell you that he wasn't alone at the time. I carry the feeling that his friend who was with him had some guilt, some responsibility in my grandson's death. There's nothing I can do about that to make it right except live with the philosophy that what goes around, comes around. That's out of my hands. As far as my grandson goes, I feel he's in a better place than when he was here.

This was almost three years ago, and my daughter, his mother, is still having a very hard time. I know that I did the best I could but because I helped raise him I have my own guilt. I often wonder if I did everything I could to prevent such a tragic end to his young life. Yet if I wallow in self pity and carry overwhelming guilt, it won't change the reality of the outcome of this tragedy.

As I listened to Mildred reflect on her encounter with cancer and other physical problems and the sadness of her grandson's life and tragic death, I wanted to know something about how she was able to move past those potentially paralyzing times.

There are times when I met with a counselor and again with a therapist to get some help with looking at situations in my life differently, rather than succumbing to depression. One of those times was when I had taken on the responsibility of caring for my young grandson, who was two years old, and my mother-in-law was also dying. I guess it was too much for me. I just picked up and left one day and didn't come back home overnight. I was overwhelmed and I just ran away from it all. I realized then that I needed help.

Talking with a therapist about it all gave me another perspective. When my daughter left the country abruptly and my grandson's father didn't take care of the child, I ended up with all the responsibility but none of the authority. I look back on that situation now and realize I should have gotten legal custody of my grandson rather than struggling with the unpredictability of his parents. In therapy I learned to set my own parameters. I was able to look at the situation in a way where I no longer felt responsible for solving everyone's problems.

Now in my 70's I've finally learned how to accept what life has brought me and avoid falling into depression.......I've learned to live without regrets."

I reached the point finally where I could no longer tolerate having my daughter and grandson moving in and out as they pleased. I set a time for them to move into a place of their own and there was no negotiation on that. I guess at that point I was ready to accept the consequences of my decision and the action I took. I did have some guilt later but as I look back on it I think I did the best I could, for me and for them.

Thankfully, now that I'm in my 70's, I've finally learned how to accept what life has brought me and avoid falling into depression. It's no longer part of my life to let myself be bogged down by "should-haves," "could haves" and regrets. I've learned to live without regrets. That was hard for me to do but a very important part of my growth. I may not like some parts of my life but if I dwell on them it saps my energy and leaves me frustrated. There are things in my life now that I've accepted and learned to live with. One of those situations is my marriage.

It's hard for me to talk about this kind of personal stuff but I'll be as open with you as I can. My husband and I are like roommates. We don't have an intimacy. I like him, he's an honorable man, but we don't really share our lives. My husband and I eat meals together but not much else. I do my things and he just stays at home. Many of his friends have died and he doesn't seem to want to make new ones. He watches television and he reads the papers, but he rarely leaves his chair. I'd like to do more traveling and engage in more social activities but my husband is not much interested in any of that. We don't talk about feelings and personal stuff but he'll comment on the news and he'll ask, "What are we having for dinner tonight?" He's a couch potato.

I no longer go to church very much. My husband isn't interested in going and I get funny vibes when I go alone. Most everyone there is part of a couple. My husband and I don't do much together anymore. I tried to interest him in things for a long time and then I gave up. My husband can take ten naps and still have no trouble sleeping at night. I think its boredom.

I used to get angry but I don't any more. I just go ahead and do my things and make a separate life for myself. My husband doesn't give me any birthday presents, or Christmas gifts or remember our anniversary. I used to feel a lot of hurt, frustration, sadness and disappointment but I realized I couldn't change him, only change my attitude to acceptance. I have no expectations any more. I know I can't depend on him for emotional support so I get that from friends and family and from myself. I've come to accept that situation for what it is and go on with my life.

One of the things that gives me great pleasure and satisfaction and adds meaning to my life is the sense of accomplishment I get from making things. I create objects that are beautiful and useful—

quilts, furniture covers, and other things, mostly for a home. I love quilting and creating with fabric. People like what I create and it feeds my sense of worth. I feel good when I get praise or compliments.

Sometimes people call me an artist but I think of myself more as a crafts person.

I make a lot of things for my family. I've made six quilts these past five months and given them all away... After all, how many can I use? I make smaller things too, like table runners, hot pad mitts, curtains and Christmas decorations. And as my grandchildren get married I've made all the wedding dresses. I guess it's my nature to enjoy giving things to people.

I have another hobby too. I've enjoyed making scrap books for each of my children and grandchildren and they've expressed pleasure in getting them. The books have pictures of grandparents, great grandparents and other relatives, as well as other photos and memorabilia, correspondence and small objects. I've done eight books for my daughter and her family. Each is about 90 pages long so that's a considerable project.

I don't feel like I've failed at something but that I've learned what isn't for me.

I also get pleasure from learning new things on my computer. I take classes to learn to do different things. I love to cook and to garden too. I like the feeling of getting dirt under my fingernails. I've taken an art class and a writing class. I wasn't really very good at some of the things but it was fun to try them out. I don't feel like I've failed at something but that I've learned what isn't for me. The creative things that I spend my time on are very, very important to me. I love making things and learning things.

I like to read books. It's amazing the amount of information I get from the characters in the stories I read. I learn about their emotions, how they think, how they relate to other people and how they feel about their lives. I actually learn about myself, how I might react in some situations, how others handle disappointments, challenges, and other things. Many stories show you that one person can really make a difference in the world and those kinds of stories are inspiring and uplifting for me.

I enjoy being with people. I like the dialogue, the give and take, the social experience. I hope when I'm gone I'll be remembered as a friend, a nice person, and that I'm faithful and responsible. At this time in my life, I'm truly enjoying every day. I've learned how to do that and I get pleasure from the simple things. I've learned a lot living these seventy plus years. Sure there have been setbacks and unexpected challenges. I've learned that life has its valleys that I have to get through and then I enjoy and appreciate the peaks, the good times. Each day that I'm here and in reasonable health is a blessing.

I'm not going to spend any time or energy taking on whatever worries may come next week. I might not even be here. I'm here now and today my life is good. My wisdom, if you want to call it that, has been learning to look at what comes my way every day and asking myself "Is my glass half full or half empty"? I see every day as a blessing, good or bad, it's a blessing.

You have to count on living every single day
in a way you believe will make you feel good
about your life, so that if it were over tomorrow
you'd be content.
— Jane Seymour

AFTERTHOUGHTS

For me, eight simple words in my conversation with Mary continue to be an enormous gift of insight and wisdom. After talking with her I've found myself silently asking myself her simple question, "Is my glass half full or half empty?" My answer to that question has the power to change how I handle almost all situations and challenges, both little and big. This is a life lesson that I, for one, often forget or neglect. It takes a conscious effort to react to things philosophically instead of emotionally. Yet it can make an enormous difference in my life—and most probably yours as well—to look at that glass half empty instead of making a choice to define a particular situation as a glass that's half full.

Many years ago a friend said to me, "You know, it's not so much what happens to you as how you deal with it." In many ways that remark embraces the same philosophy, the same wisdom. Bad things do happen to good people, as the well known expression goes. Much of life is out of our control. However, we are in control of how we react to events and people in our lives.

Blythe (age 52)

The count of those who have lost their jobs recently grows daily. Many emotional and psychological losses come with the loss of a job. Possibly it's the end of a promising career, loss of income and status, opening the door to anxiety, depression, fear, insecurity and other negative emotions that threaten health and self-image. Each person in that situation has their own challenges to face depending on the individual situation. Blythe's story is one of many. Even if you can't relate to the specifics of her situation, you probably can identify and empathize with some of her challenges, and her resilience and determination in facing them. I hope that by the time her story appears in print, these challenges will not only have been faced, but overcome.

> *The most satisfying thing in life*
> *is to have been able to give*
> *a large part of one's self to others*
>
> – Pierre Teilhard de Chardin

I'm more sure of who I used to be than of who I am now. I don't know how to think of myself not being able to continue the work I loved. My job disappeared when the funding dried up for my position. I was very attached to the job I held for the past six years at a not-for-profit agency, working with older people who

34

lived in the neighborhood. Our agency provided a social situation for these people, many of whom lived pretty much in isolated situations. I think older persons are a neglected and misunderstood population, particularly low-income elders. I've always liked hanging around with older people because I learn a lot. In my job I served our older population in many ways—preparing and delivering meals, organizing group activities, and running caregiver support sessions. The seniors I've worked with are interesting, creative and often very wise. Interacting with people in their 70's, 80's and 90's has taught me a lot. I also felt I was doing something helpful and meaningful for others. My work gave me deep satisfaction and a feeling of being connected to something bigger than myself. Now I feel like part of me is missing.

The seniors I've worked with are interesting, creative and often very wise. Interacting with people in their 70's, 80's and 90's has taught me a lot.

Right after my job was terminated I got a cold, bronchitis and other complications. No surprise, eh? It gets you when you're down. Not only was I depressed but I couldn't breathe deeply without summoning a coughing spell. When I went out of my apartment I concentrated on keeping a smile on my face. It's amazing how differently people on the street respond to me when I'm smiling. It's contagious. The smiles come very readily to me. My exterior smile affects my interior mood and has helped get me through some tough weeks of poor health and fruitless job searching. I've spent a lot of time thinking about how to re-invent myself; to figure out the very thing you asked, "Who am I now that I'm not who I was?" What my life was is gone. I didn't shed my identity, it was taken from me.

One of the most satisfying things I was able to bring into my work at the agency was Laughter Yoga, a practice that has become a life-line for me. I became familiar with it when I was looking for a way to cheer up some of the older people I worked with. Laughter Yoga is a combination of yogic breathing and laughter. It was created by Dr. Madan Kataria, an Indian physician from Mumbai. He started the first laughter group with just five people. Now it's a worldwide phenomenon with social laughter clubs in more than 60 countries. It was amazing to see the senior groups I worked with enjoying laughing and actually acting playful. In addition to the classes I offered, I worked with the older people on bringing humor and some lightness into their lives outside of class. I told them to look around, there's humor everywhere. Children laugh about 400 times a day; adults average about 12 times a day. Many older persons have forgotten how to laugh.

There aren't any jokes in laughter yoga, it's not humor dependent. It doesn't rely on jokes, just joyous laughter, deep breathing and chanting like yo-ho-ho, ha-ha-ha coordinated with the breathing exercises. The body doesn't know the difference between spontaneous laughter and simulated laughter. Both open up your chest. It's very rigorous but very exhilarating. There are a myriad of health benefits from laughter yoga; it's very good for asthmatics. It strengthens the immune system, releases endorphins and stress hormones. It also lowers blood pressure, reduces anxiety, enhances deeper breathing, and I believe it increases a person's productivity and creativity. I've found that it's a fun, feel-good group activity and a powerful antidote for depression. Laughter yoga is actually a cardio-vascular workout and burns about 300 calories an hour. It's not much different from the result you get from a workout at the gym.

I know that laughter yoga has made a difference in my personal life, as well as to those who've taken classes from me. It allows me to laugh in the face of adversity, trust my playful, humorous instincts and be downright silly. In these times of personal frustration and stress I fall back on my laughter exercises. I make a point of doing my laughter yoga every day. It has been important to me in so many ways. It's helped me with my sexuality, accept my body, and realize that I'm attractive and graceful. I've also been able to deal honestly with my lifetime eating disorder, binge eating. This is all as a result of laughter yoga. Now I'm no longer connected to either of the two communities that meant a great deal to me—the social service agency where I worked with the seniors, and the space where I did my Laughter Yoga classes with the seniors.

These days, as I don't have a job, I've discovered that doing volunteer work really takes me outside of myself. When I'm giving back and helping others I feel great. I've also started volunteering at a wellness club for people who have cancer and their caregivers as well. I lead stress reduction Laughter Yoga workshops there and also at a local hospital for patients and their families. This is very rewarding work for me. It's all about connecting to people, making a difference for them and for me. I thrive on serving people, helping people, laughing with people. I'm now getting requests from senior centers, hospitals, community groups and some corporations. I've been doing quite a bit of self-promotion for laughter yoga presentations in recent weeks and several of them are paying me a few hundred dollars. If I can get more of this kind of work I might only have to get a part-time job for some regular income. I need a paycheck and this is mostly volunteer work but I get a lot of satisfaction and good feelings back in place of money.

Blythe lives in a two-bedroom rented apartment. She's taken a roommate who shares her living area, kitchen and the rent. She's never been married.

I don't feel a need to be married at this time of my life but I would like a comfortable, caring, close and committed relationship. I did have regrets a number of years back when some of my friends were having babies. I knew if I didn't have children then that I never would. Now I'm 53 and over that stage and no longer have a desire for children. I do regret that I never met a man that I could really fall in love with. I guess I'm romantic but I still believe in the magic and miracle of falling in love—but marriage? I don't think so. I'm so used to being on my own that if I'm alone the remainder of my life, I know I'll be OK. My most immediate need now isn't a relationship, its finding employment.

The reality is that the economy at this time is in a bad way, particularly for non-profit and social work agencies. There's no money out there to fund projects to help older folks on limited incomes. The only thing I can do while I search for employment is try to get gigs for my laughter yoga sessions. We all can use laughter in these tough times. I want very much to continue that work but when the unemployment checks stop in six months I'll need a job. I'm doing what I can to keep from feeling hopeless and depressed but prospects aren't good out there. Looking for a job can be a long and unrewarding process, but getting angry, depressed or acting and feeling like a victim doesn't get me anywhere. I've learned to take a positive stance and ask myself, "How can I grow from this?"

It wasn't a surprise to hear Blithe talk about continuing to grow. Earlier in our conversation she described how in past years she worked hard to deal with several limitations and disabilities. Blithe has learned to compensate, explore substitute behaviors and continue to grow in spite of a personal problems and limitations.

I'll probably always have a binge eating disorder. My challenge is to accept it and control it. I'm a full-figured woman and when my weight is controlled I look good and feel good. I've been using food for comfort since I was three years old. As a child my metabolism burned it off. When I came into my mid-thirties I didn't burn it off any more and I became very overweight. When people are addicted to drugs, alcohol or cigarettes they don't have to deal with those addictions except by choice. With food it's different. You have to eat every day. Food addiction is the most difficult kind of recovery. Anorexia, bulimia, binge eating disorder—these are all more complicated and more difficult to recover from.

It has taken me many years to accept that I will always have this eating disorder and I owe it to myself to control it. It's my responsibility. As long as I'm not binging every day of my life, which I used to do, I allow myself to binge one day a week, and I forgive myself for that. I make no excuses. I live with this addiction and my challenge is to control it. As long as I keep exercising, as long as I can hold a job, as long as I can hold on to relationships, then it's OK. I can live with the self-imposed discipline of controlling it. I know what need it serves, it fills up the emotional hole inside.

When I was growing up I realized that I had some kind of limitation that prevented me from learning the way most people do. My parents called me stupid. It took me a long time to discover that it wasn't stupidity but some form of a learning disability. I could read slowly but I didn't do it well or very often. I didn't get any encouragement or support at home or from my teachers. I cut classes in school because I couldn't learn at the pace of my classmates, couldn't do homework well, and had enormous frustration writing a paper. I read very slowly, so doing research was a real challenge, and organizing my thoughts and writing a paper was close to impossible for me. However, I realized that I had very good analytical skills, and was able to devise creative ways to handle what I couldn't do writing and reading. I also came to realize that my senses and my intuition were heightened.

I never considered myself a creative person when I was younger. Now, as an adult, I write poetry often and I decorate mirrors with shells, make decorative boxes and picture frames. I don't consider myself an artist but I am a creative person. Creative expression is vital for me, and for everyone in their own way. Staying creative is a lifeline. For me it isn't the final product that matters, it's the process.

What I learned from working with older people is that many who never thought of themselves as creative started painting, writing, and telling stories because I was able to encourage them to try. With acceptance and encouragement they dared to explore what they could do, what they could enjoy, what they could create. I've observed that this sense of freedom and liberation seems to come with age. When we're younger we listen to other voices. Older people are often free to listen to their own inner voice. Of course some people get stuck in old patterns and fear of change. And then there are those who are dealing with illnesses, pain or disability and can't seem to reach beyond those limitations. Yet I think of an older gentleman I knew who didn't have the use of his arms so he learned to paint holding the brush in his mouth. A person can move beyond their limitations. I have.

Although all of my friends went on to college after high school, I couldn't even attempt that. I decided to look for a job. I was very gregarious, outgoing, attractive, and always had lots of friends. Those qualities helped me get a job as a talent and casting agent in the entertainment industry. They let me do what I was good at, things like putting together interesting events, getting the agency press coverage, and dealing with the clients face to face. They understood that I couldn't type or handle administrative things.

What I learned from working with older people is that many who never thought of themselves as creative started painting, writing, and telling stories because I was able to encourage them to try.

But after eight years at that job the work no longer gave me satisfaction. I began a stretch of binge eating. That's when I got in touch with my emotions for the first time and decided to join Overeaters Anonymous.

I left my job, took some time off, and gave a lot of thought to what I could do without a college education that would be satisfying, creative, and useful. What really resonated with me and was close to my heart was serving people. I saw that seniors, especially older persons with low incomes, were often a neglected population in the city I live in. I really wanted to do something that could help make life better for them.

I knew that with my limitations I wouldn't be able to get into a four year university program, much less complete a master's program in social work. A friend suggested that I probably could get a certificate in gerontology and after deliberating for several years, I decided to try, in spite of my learning disabilities. I hoped to get certified in both art therapy and gerontology. I was pleased that they gave me credit for experiential service I had done in the community. I also got credit for the work at the casting agency that taught me a lot about working with people. When it came to writing papers I hit a brick wall. I was able to convince my instructors to let me do the assignments for papers orally. I was able to get those certifications because they made that concession for me. I have an undergraduate degree in community and human services, and counseling and certificates in art therapy and laughter therapy.

The position I held for these past six years didn't require the graduate level of educational requirements in social work or gerontology, which is why I was able to quality for it. Now the positions available in the area of serving older persons all require educational degrees I don't have.

Today a meaningful job working exclusively with older people might be impossible for me to find. I hope I can utilize my laughter skills and keep myself out of depression. It's important for me to do something positive every day for myself. I'm determined to take responsibility for my physical and emotional health; I smile, laugh, make good food choices, connect to people, serve others. And at the end of each day I ask myself, What were the positives in this day? I'm most often able to find an answer that.

I need a job because I need an income. If I assess my situation realistically, I'm potentially facing a financial crisis. There are days when the fear kicks in and other days when I feel hopeful and get a new surge of energy. During these past days I've thought of all sorts of things, including ways to start doing my own thing by making laughter yoga a full time enterprise. I work at how I can market myself and my laughter therapy workshops. I'm planting seeds by contacting several press venues with the hope of media attention that would give my laughter yoga workshops a jump start. I suppose when my unemployment benefits run out I'll have to settle for anything that will replace that loss of income, even if it means taking your hamburger order at Burger King!

It's faith in something and enthusiasm for something that makes life worth living.

– Oliver Wendell Holmes

AFTERTHOUGHTS

In addition to the immediate problem of dealing with the loss of her job, Blythe's eating disorder and learning disabilities remain life-long challenges. Those specifics describe her particular situation, yet each of us may face our own new crisis along with our exiting problems and limitations. It can be a time of potentially devastating confusion and overload. It also might be an opportunity to strengthen resolve, seek new avenues of interest and possible work, and re-order priorities. Blythe has experienced deep satisfaction from doing her Laughter Yoga workshops for older persons, cancer patients and their caregivers, and hospital patients and their families. She has new resolve to promote her workshops and produce modest income from those efforts. Declaring she doesn't need a large income, a part time regular job along with the workshops might well cover her needs.

As unemployment is rising daily in all businesses and

professions, none of us know when or if we might face the need to seek work or grow work out of a personal passion as Blythe is doing. During this process she is taking positive steps to eat sensibly, exercise and keep her attitude positive. The specifics of her situation may be far different from yours or mine, yet there is much to be learned from Blythe's story. Life lessons often come in disguise.

Sal (age 77)

Follow the voice of your spirit
Remember to dream
Listen to the wisdom of your soul
Dance to the music of your heart.

                                – Anonymous

Because women really enjoy spending a long lunch and good conversation with other women, a friend of mine has set up one day a month when a number of friends and acquaintances are invited to join what she's labeled The Ladies Who Lunch. It was at one of those lunches that I met Sal, an energetic and engaging woman of 77 who had stopped by the luncheon on the way home from her dance group. She told me with great animation that dance and movement had become a major activity in her life. That same lively essence was present when I was invited to her home a few weeks later—a charming place with high ceilings and wonderful old wood floors. The walls were abundant with art, and photographs of friends and family filled the shelves and bookcases.

When we sat down to have our conversation, Sal said with gusto, "Let me tell you how dancing came into my life." And so she began.

I was at a conference on positive aging. A woman came up to me seemingly out of nowhere and said, "I have to talk with you about something very important." Because I had worked for many years as a grants officer in the arts division of a local foundation, I was used to such encounters, and I was sure that she wanted an introduction to someone at the foundation who could help her get funding. But that wasn't what she wanted at all. She wanted me to come to her group and dance. I told her I wasn't a dancer, had never danced, and had no interest in joining her group. She then told me her name and explained that she was the founder of her group. I recognized her name and I knew she had a national reputation.

There had been stories in the newspapers about a 99-year-old once-professional performer who was now doing choreography for a local group. They were stimulated and excited to work with this energetic older dancer, and she, in turn, was pleased to get another opportunity to draw upon her talents—to be alive again. She had recently created a piece for the group that needed four women of different ages. They had already selected dancers who were in their 30's, 40's, and 50's—one for each decade—but they needed a tall, gray-haired older lady to complete the ensemble. When the founder saw me at the conference I struck her as visually perfect for the piece. She assured me that I could learn the dance steps. So I came to a rehearsal of her group the next day.

At the rehearsal, the other three women caught on to the steps immediately, but I had to keep re-doing them. I'd mess it up and then try again, and again. I kept routing the instructions for the steps from my brain down to my body. The choreographer kept saying, "Just keep doing it, don't worry, your body will teach you." That seemed so different from how I've learned all my life. My mind has always told my body to listen to it. My body took instructions from what was inside my head. I was trying to remember things like two steps right, one step left, turn right. My mind heard those instructions and was trying to get the messages to my body. Finally, I somehow let my body take over, kept my mind out of it the best I could, and began to learn the routine by just letting my body move. And as my body took over, my intellect began to sit back and watch. I stopped counting, I quit trying to remember the sequence of step, I let my mind let go and my body took over.

I was a beginner and I loved it. I didn't have to be the expert, which is the role I'd felt compelled to play in all of my old jobs. Never having danced before, I could begin learning from an empty slate. And it was very exciting for me. I can honestly say that I love the group and I love to dance. It has become a very important part of my life. It's obvious to me that everyone in the whole group loves to dance as much as I do. The group is very

I was a beginner and I loved it. I didn't have to be the expert, which is the role I'd felt compelled to play in all of my old jobs.

close. We meet often during the week and either enjoy learning new steps, or often we go to retirement residences, Alzheimer's units, and other places in the community that invite us. Sometimes we perform for an audience or persons in those memory loss units or in retirement residences, and often we hold hands and dance with the people who invited us.

I'll tell you a wonderful story about the day a small group of us were scheduled to visit a special Alzheimer's unit. I got there about half an hour before the rest of the group. I had been listening to music on my car radio and my body was sort of moving with the music when I got out of the car. I walked into the room where about ten of the patients were already seated in chairs waiting for us. I was still sort of moving in dance steps to the music in my head. I was kind of singing, humming and moving my body. They were all sitting there looking numb. I was clicking my fingers and some of them started doing that with me, a couple of others opened their eyes, and some of them started moving their shoulders. It took time but somehow there was a physical response and an awareness from some of them. That incident was just a marvel to me. I love bringing music, movement, and dance to Alzheimer's patients. At this time of my life I'm really celebrating the new things that are coming into my life—music, dance, performing, and getting the pleasure and satisfaction of bringing those things to others.

I've gained a deeper insight from a mutual friend into Sal's satisfaction with the visible response from those memory loss patients. Her father had suffered with extreme dementia and rarely responded to a room full of caring relatives. I'm sure Sal would have hummed a melody and danced for her father if she had known that it might trigger a response from him.

When Sal and I talked she did tell me how she feared that her father's illness made her prone to a similar pattern of loss. She related her experience and how she dealt with the disability and its aftermath.

I had a mini-stroke. I was in an unfortunate situation when it happened. I was driving across country on a five-week trip to visit my sons and their families. I enjoy driving the back roads because I love being out in the country. The day I started the trip a fierce rainstorm came up and a drive that should have taken me five hours took a lot longer. It was a hard and exhausting trip and I went to sleep immediately when I reached my son's home. When I went into the kitchen the next morning I said good morning to my daughter-in-law. I thought that was what I had said, but it came out like I was babbling; when I tried speaking again it was even worse, not one intelligible word. So I stopped talking and just smiled at my daughter-in-law when she left for work.

I felt physically fine, yet when I tried to speak again, nothing came out of my mouth, not a word. I was terrified. I didn't know what to do. I decided to drive to the local library. I sat by a window that overlooked a lake for many hours thinking that I had the beginning of Alzheimer's. When I realized it was time for me to go home I went to check out a book. When I spoke a few words to the librarian my words came out in normal speech. The immediate crisis was over. It wasn't until I was back home from my visit that I went to the doctor. His diagnosis was that I had had a mini-stroke. I was left with relief that it wasn't early Alzheimer's but anxiety over having been left with a problem of not being able to recall the names of objects and places. I was told that there was a change in my brain function as I had lost a considerable amount of neurons.

I live with that limitation now. At first I was furious, then I became agitated, after a time I was getting along pretty normally, even joking about my forgetting, and then I just let it go. Now it's one of the limitations I just live with. I've learned to let go of other things too. I'm losing some of my eyesight, my hearing, and my hair seems to be slowly falling out. I've made those things secondary to what I'm learning about my emotions and my mind. I'm also finding out new things about my body that I never knew and I'm learning new ways of thinking.

With my loss of words I could no longer do crossword puzzles. I had a habit of doing the daily crossword in the newspaper. At first I was struggling to get my memory back to making my brain work the way it used to. Finally I realized that I had to let it go. The exciting thing is that I've discovered a new way to approach the puzzles. When I look at the clues, I no longer try to think consciously of what word they're hinting at. I just look at the word that asks the question and I don't try to think of an answer. I just wait until the answer comes into my consciousness. I don't know how to describe the process but I've completely let go of thinking, of using my mind consciously to seek the answers. I've opened up to doing many things in different ways, and as a result, new interests have opened up for me.

When Sal described her unique adjustment to the changes resulting from the mini-stroke, I asked if she had ever dealt with other health challenges. She volunteered the story of her first marriage, the end of it, and what followed.

He was in his mid-20's and I had just turned 17. We were married, settled down, and had three healthy sons, although I had several miscarriages and twin girls that didn't survive. We were married for 16 years. I loved him but his behavior became aggressive and erratic and he absolutely refused any psychological help. There were many reasons that our marriage fell apart. It was sad and it was hard for me to leave him. We eventually were divorced; it was a terrible time in my life. I agonized about leaving my husband, about who was going to have custody of the children, which one of us could stay in the house, and those conflicts took a toll on me and my body.

I hadn't been to a doctor for more than five years so I thought I'd better check out my health, as I felt totally exhausted. I remember going to the doctor's office and that's the last thing I recalled until I woke up in the hospital with tubes in me, bandages on me, and everyone in my family sitting around the room. I had cancer in my throat and my thyroid glands. I'm certain that

I remember going to the doctor's office and that's the last thing I recalled until I woke up in the hospital with tubes in me, bandages on me, and everyone in my family sitting around the room.

the stress and emotional turmoil at that time was a factor in my illness. Thankfully I've never had a reoccurrence.

When I had recovered sufficiently I decided to go to work. As a younger person I loved to draw and paint. I always felt like I had the innate talent to be an artist but I gave up my plans to study in favor of my early marriage. Art was still of enormous interest to me so I took a job at our local art museum. At the time I was fascinated with film and filmmakers and I suggested to the head of the museum they should have a film department. At that time there was only one museum in the country that had one, the Museum of Modern Art in New York. I went there for a day to meet the people at MOMA, got acquainted with their collection, met several *avant-guard* filmmakers and felt ready to move ahead. My boss told me to set up anything I wanted so I went to a couple of foundations and they all gave the museum money to proceed with my plan.

I loved my work, it was exciting and fun, but after it was established as a regular focus of the museum programs it didn't interest me just to manage it. The creative part of my work was over, and I decided to leave my job. Then, unexpectedly, I got an offer to run the film program in another city for one year. I thought that would be perfect, I could handle a short commitment, and the city itself was well-known for its sophisticated cultural life.

In the course of that year I got to know a photographer whose work I admired. We began caring a great deal for each other but I resisted the idea of marriage. I was 15 years older than him. I told him that we were in different stages of our lives, that there would be a time when he'd want to have children and I was through with that part of my life. But he pursued me and wouldn't take no for an answer. We had a wonderful marriage and he developed a brilliant career, not only with his photography but also as a writer and film-maker.

My next work opportunity came from a foundation in the city I had relocated to. That city is home to me now, I'm still here. The job involved dispensing grants to groups and individuals in literature and the visual arts. During my years at the foundation I expanded their areas of giving to include music, dance, film, photography and theatre. I loved the work and stayed on at the foundation for 16 years. When I was 65 I decided to retire.

During my later years at the foundation, and my purview expanded, I was given an assistant. I hired a smart and charming young woman; we worked closely together and also became personal friends. My husband was always hanging around and helping with the film and photography programs. The three of us worked together for the last two years before my retirement. Then, exactly as I feared it might, my husband who was so much younger than I, fell in love with my assistant. He said he wanted to reconcile but I could tell he was tortured over making that decision so we parted and were divorced. He and my assistant married and moved to Paris.

Though both of them tried to maintain a relationship with me, it was too painful for me and I cut them off totally. For more than two years we had no contact at all. One day—I can't explain how this happened—but the pain of it all was over. I realized that I wasn't in love with him anymore. I'll always love him and I love her too, they're both very special to me, but I no longer am 'in love.'

I wrote them a letter and told them how I felt. My ex-husband called the day my letter arrived to tell me on that very day, their daughter was born. They wanted me to be godmother. I said to him, "What will you say to your daughter when you tell her that this white-haired old lady was your first wife?" His reply was, "I would simply tell her that the two women I've loved most in my life are her mother and her godmother."

I know that many people in my generation wouldn't approve or understand this kind of relationship. Yet I grew up in a family that opened their home and their hearts to everyone.

I know that many people in my generation wouldn't approve or understand this kind of relationship. Yet I grew up in a family that opened their home and their hearts to everyone. I never witnessed discrimination or ill feelings towards anyone of any class, race or age. I was open to re-connecting and so now, in addition to my grown sons, I have a new family. Ours was a marriage at a certain time in our lives. We truly loved each other and I believe we will always love each other, but we are not 'in love' anymore. His wife was my dear friend and I have a love for her as well, and I dearly love their daughter. After all, I'm her godmother.

One of Sal's sons and her granddaughter were due to arrive shortly so I knew our conversation was almost over. I asked her

to talk briefly about her personal philosophy at this time of her life.

I'm really kind of excited of letting go of who I used to be. I'm learning to let go in many ways as I get older. I want to continue in my new way, learning from my whole self. I'm beginning to see what letting-go actually means in practice. That's what I was able to do with my memory problem when I allowed another part of my body to take over. So now I live alone. The older I get the more silence and solitude I crave. I go deeply inside. I'm into this earth we live on; the universe we're in. I get up at 5 and go out into the garden and weed and just look at the plants, and I take long early morning walks. There's no traffic on the street so I can hear the wind and the birds; I hear the sounds of the earth and the heavens. I'm just beginning to get into it all.

My parents were Episcopalian, yet after I was out on my own I found that my spiritual connection was more inside of myself. I became a Quaker for a while because their silence appealed to me. Now I can go to services at any church, any religion. The external traditions, symbols, services, and prayers are all interesting to me. Of course each is a totally different experience. What each of the many churches, synagogues, and meditation centers I visit touches inside of me is always the same. It has always been that way for me.

I'm loving the experience of my aging. Of course, I'm not loving some of the losses, but I'm loving what I gain, what I learn. It seems that I've discovered new ways to live with this body—not just the mind but the emotions, the physical body too. And there's the ego too. I no longer want my ego to tell me to serve it; I now want it to serve me. My ego, my old desire to control keeps wanting to take over space that I now know can be served better when I just let go. I'm trying to explain to you the feeling but I just can't seem to find the right words to describe what just letting go can give me. It's letting go of the part of the intellect, the ego, the control that I've so often gravitated to in the past. My new way is like my dance experience, where I had to let go of my controlling mind.

I have a new way of thinking in these years of my late 70's. I sort of tell my brain to sit down over here and let other parts of me deal with the new experiences. I really can't find the right words to describe how I make this happen but it works for me. I'm just beginning to catch on to this aging thing. My life in my 77th year is rich.

> *To exist is to change, to change is to mature,*
> *to mature is to go on creating oneself endlessly.*
>
> – Henri Bergson

Afterthoughts

It's wonderful to learn of Sal's new passion for dance. Yet most inspiring, I believe, was how she discovered a new way of learning, letting her body lead her mind. So often we hear the words "body" and "mind" in the same sentence but in our world they're far from equal. Our actions follow our thinking. We've been taught that the mind is, so to speak, the driver of the bus. Reversing what our schooling and life experience has taught us, putting the body first and letting go of our controlling brain, can be an amazing feat. The challenge, it seems, is to learn what new functions our bodies might learn; to understand more about our bodies and allow them new leadership in some situations. It will take some "un-learning" for our minds but the adventure might bring new rewards.

Sal's story of reconciliation with her ex-husband and his wife is, in my view, extraordinary. Coming to a place in herself where she was able to let go of her pain, anger, disappointment, embarrassment, or whatever feelings she was living with, opened the opportunity to form a meaningful bond of friendship and love. A situation that could have remained a dark pool of rejection and betrayal instead became a bright river of forgiveness and love. There are personal circumstances in many of our lives, with parents, siblings, children, employers, friends and others, that end in long-term alienation. Some situations leave no road back, yet I suspect there are circumstances where the opportunity for healing and forgiveness can be as close as reaching out one hand. Sal's particular experience of family upheaval may be far different from your own, but it can serve as an example of forgiveness, reconciliation, and the courage to move on.

Lucy (age 64)

LUCY WELCOMED ME into her home with a warm smile. I felt as if I had entered an art gallery. Surrounding me were dramatic collages, vibrant images painted on vases, glass bowls, plates and decorative frames. As Lucy led me to a table in the dining room, I noted in passing that some of the themes in her art were somber, others delightfully humorous. As we sat down in the dining room I paused to admire a painted glass bowl on the table in front of the petite, 64-year-old Lucy, who was eager to begin our conversation.

My career in art began quite a few years ago but it was only about six years ago that I started painting on glass. In the beginning I just kind of made it up. First I would ask a glass-blower to create a vase or bowl for me in a specific shape and size. Then I would visualize what I wanted to surface to look like. But because I applied the paint to the inside of the bowl, I had to apply the layers upside-down and in reverse.

For example, this piece here on the table is called The Circus. If you look at it closely you'll see that I painted the figures first. Then I painted the flowers on their clothes; next I painted the background, the layers of gold and red-orange in the sky. The last thing I painted was the layers of blue in the background. The scene is painted in reverse order, but because the bowl is clear glass, the layers appear in the correct order when viewed from the outside.

It's sort of perverse I guess, but it's similar to my career—upside down and backwards. I sort of made up my own thing. My style evolved by accident. I discovered I could do things with glass that I couldn't do with painting and now I've made a career of painting on glass. Once I've done it it's not correctable. Another media I like to work in is watercolor. You can't correct that either, which is kind of freeing. You have to just do it and let it out and let it go. I had to learn that.

I consider myself as a professional artist now but it always amazes me when I paint or when I say that out loud. I look at the piece I'm working on and I think, "Wow, I did that!" It irritates me when someone asks me how I like retirement. I'm not exactly retired; I've started over again. I'm working full time, for myself this time.

There's no question that Lucy has become a serious and distinguished artist. Her art has been displayed in several local, national, and international exhibits as well as in more than a dozen juried art shows.

Lucy's first career was very different. She earned a graduate degree in sociology and spent many years as a professor at a state university, followed by a stretch of time working as a research scientist and investigator of health related issues. Her major interests were in aging, family relationships, older volunteers, and health research. She's the author of three books in her field and a Fellow of the Gerontological Society of America for "distinguished contributions to the field of aging."

As I look back on my younger days, it seems to me that I might have begun to pursue a career in art earlier, were it not for one or two fortuitous circumstances. Although I had a strong desire to study art, I thought that most probably I couldn't make a living as an artist so I made a sensible decision to go in the other direction. At that time, my father had retired and was going through a difficult time. I wanted to study older people because I believed, at that time, with some naïveté, that retirement was the cause of the difficulties he was having. In fact, as I realized much later, his behavior was erratic because of progressive dementia.

I decided to go back to the university, get my doctorate in sociology, and study older persons in retirement to reach a better understanding of human development in the later years. My sociology degree led me into my career of teaching at the university, studying some aging issues in depth and writing a couple of books. During the last years of that career I participated in several research projects, which I really enjoyed. I've come to see some parallels between those activities and my current artistic projects. For one thing, both are all-consuming creative endeavors that require substantial blocks of time to generate focus and concentration.

During all those years in academia I didn't really paint very much, but I never lost interest. My mother-in-law was a wonderful artist; she was really my teacher. I would sometimes take a couple of weeks vacation to visit her and just paint the whole time. Then I'd go back to my life at the university.

A decade ago my husband had a heart attack while we were on a vacation—I now think of it as the worst vacation I ever had. We were walking up a hill and he started to complain about chest pains and having trouble breathing. We went to a clinic and he was diagnosed as having had a heart attack. They transferred him by helicopter to a nearby hospital where he had triple by-pass surgery.

When something like this happens, it reminds you that we humans have only a finite time here on earth. My husband and I began to think seriously about what we wanted to do, how we wanted to live the rest of our lives.

I was in my late 50's when I started my career as an artist. That was almost 15 years ago. I felt a deep need to be spending some of my life just doing art. Even if I never made a living out of it, I absolutely needed to do it. I left my position, gave up my salary, and we were down to living on one income. We had some savings, and at the time my husband's business, financial planning, was really taking off. There had been times when the shoe had been on the other foot, with him not earning very much while I was drawing a good salary. We're not big spenders so the change in our living standard wasn't dramatic.

I have several role models as I moved in this new direction. I've already mentioned my mother-in-law, who is a painter; my cousin is a writer and a painter, and my brother was an artist, photographer and a writer. He died quite young—he was only 31—but he's alive inside of me. I grew up thinking I'd be an artist and a writer because that's what he did and I looked up to him. I guess I'm kind of haunted by him. I don't mean that as a negative thing. His presence remains a major influence in my life and I feel nurtured by his memory. When I do my art, it's like doing it for him too. It's like he's alive within me.

At first I painted in the basement. I set up some old cabinets, counter tops and florescent lights left from when we re-modeled our kitchen. That was a great improvement over painting here on my dining room table. But the basement was damp, it lacked good lighting, and it was not so healthy being down there all the time.

One day a friend and I were in my living room and she commented, "This is a lovely house, so full of light, and you're always down the basement." Her remark prompted my decision to transform my upstairs office into my studio. It solidified my transformation from one career to another.

The move from the basement into my study meant getting rid of almost all of my professional journals and most of my books. I donated my gerontology journals to the research center where I had worked. I kept a small number of books that would

One day a friend and I were in my living room and she commented, "This is a lovely house, so full of light, and you're always down the basement."

fit on a few shelves in my closet. This transformation of space was like a dissection. I was an artist now, not a sociologist.

I discovered very quickly that one of the features of being an artist is that I would always be doing my work alone. In my other career I was surrounded by colleagues and students. At first I really liked being alone, planning my own work schedule, and no longer having a commute to work and deal with traffic. I painted in solitude with my dog at my feet. I've always been self-motivated so being productive on my own has never been a problem, but there were times when I felt lonely. Yet I soon discovered that when I made an effort to schedule activities that brought other people back into my life, it took away from my work and disrupted my concentration. Clearly, I needed to establish some kind of balance between these two spheres.

In the early days of my art career, I had very little involvement with the professional art community, though I knew I needed to develop some connections to that world. I enrolled in an art mentorship program through a local women's art registry. I also formed two art groups on my own. One was with local women artists whose art focused on aging. The other group I organized was a Jewish women's art circle that includes nationally and internationally known artists. (I'm religious and I consider myself spiritual as well.) These two groups helped to introduce me to the broader art world.

I often use Jewish themes in my art, and I meet regularly with 18 Jewish women artists to study Jewish sources. We currently have a traveling show of our work at a local synagogue; previously it was at our state university, a suburban civic center, and also a church in this area.

The first theme we worked on was Jewish women and prayer. The one we're working on now is the soul. It's a non-visual theme, which we're each using to express something personal through our art. My piece is a large glass bowl with many figures dancing around it. I call it The Community of Souls. All the figures are hand in hand and also connected by a thread that holds them together.

I'm doing more small exhibits these days and exhibiting in fewer art fairs. It's hard work to pack up my art, unpack it, and pack it up again once the show is over. Not to mention setting up and taking down the booth at each new location and battling the weather. Maybe I'm not hungry enough to keep doing those art fairs. The last one I showed at was an outdoor venue. A wind storm came up and I was literally holding the sides of my tents to keep it from falling over. I realize this isn't what I got into the art business to do. I think I'll sell my tent and only show at indoor events. Selling my work is important because it enables me to set up a relationship with people. Often when I see them again they tell me stories of how they treasure the piece they bought from me and also how their friends respond to the piece. It's really gratifying having people who want to buy my work.

A few years ago I taught some art classes in an older adults program. I noticed immediately that everybody has their own distinctive style in expressing themselves; there's something that's uniquely you that comes out when you paint. Trying out a new way of expressing oneself creatively is, in a way, like learning a new language. It's the language of art. And if you try things that you've never tried before in this new language, sometimes you discover things about yourself. Talents or interests you might never have discovered otherwise.

I'd like everyone to realize that if its dance or writing or music or visual art—sometimes your hands need to talk, or your voice, or your body. There are different parts of your body that need to express what's inside of you. There's a different kind of intelligence and some of that comes out through a form of artistic expression—a spiritual intelligence. And the truth is they've found that when you're older, if you continue to learn and be creative, you grow more dendrites and part of your mind expands. The trees that are growing out of the woman's head in this painting that I'm working on represent that expansion and continuing growth.

... they've found that when you're older, if you continue to learn and be creative, you grow more dendrites and part of your mind expands.

These days my art focuses on the theme of aging. That's where my life is now. This new work integrates my experience, my former professional interests, and what I want to be saying in my art. Continuing to be creative is one of the keys for me. And having a spiritual life that includes art has given me a good feeling about my aging. It doesn't matter that my face is getting wrinkled, I have my art and that's more important for me to have than a youthful face. I was never a young, beautiful thing. I didn't have youthful physical beauty to lose. I thrived on thinking, learning, and creating, and those are things I take with me into later life.

I'm 64 now and I often feel some ambivalence about my aging. I think about the John Lennon song with the line, "Will you still need me, will you still feed me, when I'm 64?" I remember hearing the quote "Old age is not for sissies." I guess sometimes I feel like a sissy and don't look forward to my aging. I used to be considered an expert on aging and then I started getting older. One day I looked in the mirror and I said out loud, "Who is that? Is that really me?" I got the feeling that I had entered another age, another stage of myself. All of a sudden I realized how subtle it is; I don't have the same look, that freshness that I once saw. It had crept up on me.

My father had extreme memory loss. I guess that's my biggest fear. I've recently completed a painting that I've called The Unraveling of the Mind. My fear is that it will happen to me. This theme often comes into my work. In this piece there's a woman holding on to marbles and she's saying, "As long as I have my marbles don't call me spry!" It's the way we often see old people—cute, sweet, and spry. I don't like that attitude. We're still persons. Changes happen to our minds like I've shown in this other painting of a woman with many words floating around inside and outside of her head. I call the painting Searching for Words. I think this happens to all of us, some at a younger age, some older. We loose words, we retrieve them slowly. We can't grasp them quickly like we used to do.

My art is something I can do for my whole life. I believe I have a sort of depth and richness because I'm older now and I have more experience to build on. In these later years I really treasure the moment; I'm aware in a different way. I deal with things emotionally, intellectually and spiritually, and with ordinary experiences in a way I didn't previously. It's like being in a new place, a sort of hyper-sensitivity. I come to an awareness of a different reality and it's a good place for me. Some people talk about their talent as God-given. I wouldn't use those words but I do have a sense that there's something beyond me in the creative process than what I consciously control. Art allows me to express parts of my soul. In that sense it goes pretty deep. And yet my art also has a lot of whimsy in it.

The most important thing to me is to be really alive while I am alive. I think it's too easy to sit back and spend the days in being passive; taking things in but not really noticing, not really seeing. My goal is to spend my time here in this world being here, really *being* here. I deal with my own aging through my art. Making art is my passion, and as the years go by it has become more and more of a passion. My desire to create art is like a flame inside of me struggling to come out. I've done a couple of pieces that have fire in them. I actually feel that if I were more creative I'd burst into flames. I don't know where this feeling comes from but I'm grateful for it. I think I have a maturity in my creativity now in my later life. I use all of my experience.

> *Life is a work of art; Art is a work of life.*
>
> – Lucy Rose Fischer

Afterthoughts

We aren't all going to have the adventure of becoming a professional artist in our middle years like Lucy, or in our later years like Grandma Moses. Lucy's story reveals more than artistic ability and a rise in the professional ranks. I'm inspired,

65

and I hope you are as well, by her determination to know and understand herself, take risks and change the direction of her life, let go of who she had been, and find new purpose and meaning in her life.

Most of us associate creativity with the making of items that are both exceptional and tangible. Long ago I heard a definition of creativity that includes everyone: " It's not that the artist is a special kind of person, it's that each person is a special kind of artist."

I believe that we all have the seed of creativity within ourselves. Creativity is a state of mind, an openness to life. It's a term that can be applied to making a meal as easily as writing a poem, talking with a grandchild as well as molding a piece of clay. Our personal manifestation of creativity may take the form of a hobby, a job, a volunteer commitment, or a relationship with other human beings. Silence and simplicity can be as creative as what we label productivity. The possibilities of exploring your personal form of creativity are endless.

Phyllis (age 67)

I've learned the hard way that some poems don't rhyme, and some stories don't have a clear beginning, middle, and end. Life is about not knowing, having to change, taking the moment and making the best of it without know what's going to happen next.

— Gilda Radner

Phyllis is 67 years old. She's slim, has long gray hair, and wears big glasses. Her soft-spoken, thoughtful manner goes along with a warm smile. She looks you directly in the eye when she speaks.

Her life is kept busy by commitments to political organizations and university groups, and participation in many of the arts events scheduled in the city where she lives. When we sat down to have our conversation in her charming, well-appointed home, she immediate told me that I could better understand who she is now if she began telling me the story of who she used to be. Her journey is one of challenges, changes, and continuing growth.

My grandparents were immigrants who arrived by boat in Canada and settled there, eking out a meager living. I was born and raised in Canada, along with my two siblings; my brother was 4 years older than me and my sister was 13 years younger. My parents, a working class couple, lived in relative poverty. When I was born I don't think they had two nickels to rub together. We lived with my dad's parents for a while and then moved into what I remember as a really scary neighborhood. I remember meager and difficult circumstances. I had been born at the start of WWII and those war years were hard. Our house was always cold and often we didn't have enough to eat. I felt the full weight of my parents' poverty and struggles. I was very shy and very easily humiliated. When the kids who lived next door teased me and were mean to me it left me devastated. I retreated into myself.

At one point we moved, but our new home was no less grim than the previous one. A family with several kids lived next door. The kids didn't have any supervision.

The kids my age had more things, they dressed better, and the first day I went to school they made fun of my clothes and everybody shunned me.

One day they all ganged up on me and whipped me with a rubber skipping rope. I was 7 years old at the time. I made a decision to never play with any of those kids again and the other children in the neighborhood stayed away from me too. I was very lonely and very depressed and miserable for a long time. My early childhood was lonely and miserable.

One thing that gave me some happiness, even joy in my childhood, was a small cabin on a beautiful lake that my grandparents had gotten in exchange for money that was owed them. It was a very simple place, no indoor plumbing, but right on the lakefront. I'd get up at 5 in the morning and go walking on the beach. I'd talk with frogs, pick wild flowers, watch the sunrise, and smell the fresh air. Being able to spend part of my summers there saved my childhood. It was the one thing that saved me from deep depression.

There came a time when my parents could afford to buy a house. We moved into a neighborhood in the suburbs where it was quickly evident that everyone else had a good deal more money than we did. The kids my age had more things, they dressed better, and the first day I went to school they made fun of my clothes and everybody shunned me. I had a very lonely time in my new school and I had another time of depression.

What saved my teenage years was that I was a good student; in fact, I was the valedictorian of my class. I entered college at the age of 16. I had a scholarship and a student loan. I worked summers to pay part of my tuition and I lived at home through the entire time of my undergraduate studies and my years in medical school.

My dad influenced me to aspire to a career in medicine. He spent his whole life as a book binder but he had wanted to be a doctor. He convinced me that it was the best profession in the whole world. I wanted to be a musician but because of the economic difficulties my parents had experienced, they wanted me to have a profession that could assure me economic independence.

I had been taking piano lessons for many years. I was a very serious piano student. I practiced on the old family piano in my bedroom and I began to improvise when I was quite young. I also loved to sing and I had always been a member of my school chorus. Music was important to my dad too, he was always listening to music. My attachment to music was very deep. I loved music and it was part of life, but medical school was my path.

I graduated from college in four years and got a bachelor of science degree. Then I went into medical school for another four years. During my third year in medical school I got married. My husband was in my class in medical school. We had been married a year when we moved from Canada to the United States. We did a year of rotating internship, and then I went into psychiatry. I did five years of training in both adult and child psychiatry. That was 14 years of school after high school. Through all those years I kept my music going. That was always my joy and delight.

M y marriage didn't survive my entire psychiatry training. I had one year left. I had been married five and a half years. I don't think we really ever got to know each other in depth. The internship was around a hundred hours a week for each of us; we were working all the time. My husband was in neurology. He was a very, very serious doctor, much less inclined to have fun than I. He had done better in medical school than I did. All through medical school he was studying; I was pursuing music and new friendships. My grades were right in the middle of my class because I was convinced that I'd be a better doctor if I kept one foot solidly in the world rather than making medicine my whole life. Maybe that was a rationalization. Without the music I probably would have done better academically. Yet, when I graduated I had music in my life, a collection of good friends, and I felt strongly that I would be a very good psychiatrist.

By the time my husband and I had a chance to spend any time together, several years into our marriage, we had become quite alienated.

By the time my husband and I had a chance to spend any time together, several years into our marriage, we had become quite alienated. The only thing he wanted was to lay claim to my body. I felt his approach to me sexually was mechanical and crude. He acted as if he owned my body. I soon resisted and he became very angry. We went into therapy but we weren't getting along in other ways. There was very little tenderness and affection and the sexual relationship remained pretty awful. Actually when we had more time together the relationship grew much worse.

After a while I had an affair. It was a desperate move on my part. I had to confirm that I was a sexual being. I fell head over heels with a man who was gentle and loving. The affair lasted about six months. I did recover confidence in my sexuality and that was great. There also was intimacy and tenderness between us and that, too, was wonderful. It was great but my guilt got the better of me and I confessed to my husband. He was furious that I had given myself to another man while I had denied him.

Because I had the affair, my husband decided to file for the divorce. This was before the time of the no fault laws and he had to assign me some kind of blame. He didn't use the adultery charge but picked the least pernicious category available at that time which was mental cruelty. He brought several of our friends to the divorce hearing and they testify that he had suffered greatly as a result of living with me. The divorce was accomplished and I was the one labeled as mentally cruel. It was so unfair because I was actually the one who had suffered so much cruelty.

Everyone back home had thought our marriage was made in heaven. I had disappointed my family. My mother became very depressed. We were the beautiful, professional kids on whom all kinds of hope was riding. When we originally came to town to do our internship at a local hospital the local newspaper had done a big story on the beautiful young doctor couple. My parents had developed a close friendship with my husband's parents that totally disintegrated after the divorce. When we told his parents his mother said to me, "We gave you our golden boy and look what you've done to him." My guilt was enormous. I was 28 years old and had one year of my psychiatric training left to complete.

I suffered great emotional pain after the divorce and experienced both loss and grief in spite of the fact that the marriage wasn't good. I had deep feelings of disappointment and failure. I stayed up late at night, and to keep my mind on other things I started to paint. I also started to write music and lyrics for songs. One of the very first songs I wrote was about the divorce. I began to seek out a new group of friends who were artistically inclined and loved music and other creative activities.

I also went into therapy at that time. My sessions were three times a week. I started to explore my earlier years and events that had affected me profoundly—my early childhood isolation and rejection by almost all the children I knew, my dad's depression, his shock therapy, and the time he was close to suicide. My sister had diabetes from the age of seven and that had an effect on us all.

The first real job I had after graduation was at a child psychiatry clinic. I worked there half-time and also worked half-time the clinic's teaching hospital. It was actually like two full time jobs. I eventually became discouraged with child therapy at the clinic. Parents would bring their children in and leave them, expecting me to solve the child's problems. My efforts to involve the parents met with resistance. They wanted me to do something with the child and leave them out of it. I was told that I did well in both jobs at the clinic but I tired of the pace and eventually gave up both positions. I opened my own office and set up a private practice. My first few clients were children but the business evolved to the point where I would take only adults. From the first, I only worked 4 days a week. I had decided that I wanted as much of my life outside medicine as in it.

It was very shortly after beginning my practice when I met my now life-long-love. I had been separated and divorced for about four years at that time. I had a busy life and I really wasn't looking for a relationship. I had been writing songs and I loved doing that. I was beginning to think that I might actually be a good songwriter. I also began to take some art lessons. One day a poet I had met asked me to come to a meeting of a group of local poets who got together regularly. She had heard me sing my original songs and said my lyrics were poetry. It was at that meeting that I met Wanda. There was an immediate attraction. It's a coincidence that today is the very date of our very first meeting 35 years ago. I was surprised and totally amazed that I felt a physical attraction for a woman.

I was 32 and Wanda was 23. She's 58 now, nine years young than me. I had never thought of myself as anything but heterosexual up to that point. When Wanda and I met she was just going through a divorce. She had married because she and her husband had been high school sweethearts. They married because their marriage was expected by both families. Her husband had admitted he was gay and was having other relationships, and Wanda knew she had some attraction to women but wasn't certain about her sexuality until we met. The morning after we had our first sexual experience together I remember saying to Wanda, "Yesterday I didn't know any lesbians, today I know two!" To this day we continue to laugh about that. A few months after we met we started living together.

We had a very beautiful and intense relationship and spent most of the following year together with very little outside contact. Neither of us knew any other lesbians; we weren't public. It was 1974, there was no gay right movement anywhere, and it was a time when you stayed in the closet. In our second year we began to meet a few other women couples. It was four years before we told either of our parents. My folks had suspected it because I so often mentioned Wanda in our telephone conversations. My mother's comment was, "I had hoped you'd choose an easier life." But Wanda's parents were absolutely dismayed. It took many, many years before they would acknowledge me at all. Now, 35 years later, they've often talked about how sorry they were that they didn't accept our relationship sooner and recognize how honest and deep our feelings for each other were.

We've had our ups and downs like all couples. There was a time when I had a pretty serious illness. It was during our early years together—we had moved to a home on a farm. We were cleaning out the barn when I came down with histoplasmosis – a fungal illness that grows on chicken droppings. I was quite sick for three years. My symptoms were extreme exhaustion; I did a lot of sleeping. Wanda stuck with me the whole time. We grew very close during those years. After I recovered I cut my practice to three days a week.

Shortly after I recovered my dad died, a few years later my sister committed suicide, and four years after that my mother passed away. My sister's situation was one of the hardest things in my life. She had diabetes from the age of 7. She killed herself when she was 28. She had been intermittently terribly depressed and had many suicide attempts. Her death was very hard for me. I wrote only one song that year and it was for her. I sang it over and over again. It was very healing.

There are other concerns that are always with us. We've experienced things that have taken some of the quality out of a period in our lives. We were victims of a hate crime in one neighborhood we lived in. Three young guys came to our house in the middle of the night and completely covered our cement driveway with motor oil and left a threatening message. The repair was expensive and it took three years for the police to track down the neighborhood kids that did it—three years full of legal proceedings and mental anguish that took its toll on our relationship. Time heals and our relationship is very good now. Wanda and I were legally married in Canada five years ago on the occasion of our thirtieth year together. Maybe at some time in the future we might even retire in Canada.

Performing and composing continues to give me pleasure and satisfaction. Civic engagement has nourished me. We're both very active in peace and justice issues. We're active in Women Against Military Madness, organizations that support social responsibility, and several community groups and political campaigns that keep us active and very busy. The town we live in has a population of about thirteen thousand; some

We continue to be physically intimate and there are many, many times when the warmth and comfort and just the wordlessness in our times together feels great.

are students as there's a university here. Our neighbors, our political friends in town, as well as student groups include us, call on us to be part of activities and we feel very much part of the community. I've had a successful career and I'm thankful that I've also been able to do my music. It has saved my soul. We often perform music and sing together and we've recorded two CD's. I compose new songs all the time. Music continues to nourish me.

Wanda and I have had a really wonderful relationship all these years, in spite of times of tension, health crises, and a lot of sorrow as well. We so much enjoy each other's sense of humor. We're committed to the same kind of things; we've taken similar paths in terms of what we're interested in. We continue to be physically intimate and there are many, many times when the warmth and comfort and just the wordlessness in our times together feels great.

I've written many love songs for Wanda. I just wrote a song about being a lesbian couple living in a Midwest state where there's a constitutional amendment claiming we're not next of kin. I've written and performed other songs about our political and social concerns. Writing music, singing, and performing together has been very empowering for both of us. We do ordinary things too; exercise regularly, ride together on our bicycle built for two, bike and canoe together, and we're beginning our journey of growing old together.

I can't give specific advice to other lesbian couples, each situation is so individual. I would, however, encourage others in a same-sex relationship to be out about it. It's time to stand our ground and not allow ourselves to be humiliated or downgraded or to be considered second class citizens. Getting to know yourself and accept the reality of who you are can be a process and a challenge; a psychiatrist, psychologist or social worker can offer insight and support. Gay or lesbian identity and relationships often face unexpected challenges. I think it's even more jolting if you've come to a new identity unexpectedly as I did.

I live a very regular life—some might think of it as ordinary—even though I'm a pretty dedicated non-conformist. Now, at age 67, I no longer judge myself based on how others treat me or perceive me. I've learned from the angst of my early years and survived the upset over other people's thoughts and actions. I've come into a time of being my own person. At this time of my life I'm happier, stronger and more confident in who

I am. We're not part of an exclusive gay or lesbian community, we're an active and accepted part of our total community. We have a good life.

Don't judge any woman until you have walked
two moons in her moccasins.

– American Indian proverb

AFTERTHOUGHTS

Your story most probably is very different from what Phyllis has shared, yet it's likely that you'll find something to relate to in her story. Possibly scars of a childhood of poverty, alienation, and loneliness. Or maybe it's a problematic marriage and the pain of divorce, or an illness that interrupted an on-going career. The insight to be gleaned from this story might be that pain can heal, self-awareness can change the direction of one's life, and a productive, contented lifestyle can be maintained in spite of seemingly impossible obstacles. In contrast to many prevalent stereotypes about the lifestyles of lesbians, the story of Phyllis and Wanda's long and dedicated relationship is not so different from many others.

It's important in each of our lives to feel we belong; that we're part of a family, a relationship, a community, the place where we work, and in the neighborhood we choose to live. I believe self-acceptance comes first. We're halfway home (as the saying goes) when we can confidently and honestly repeat for ourselves Phyllis's words—"I've come into a time of being my own person."

Susan (age 60)

*You need to claim the events in your life to make
yourself yours. When you truly possess all you
have been and done, which may take some time,
you are fierce with reality.*

— Florida Scott Maxwell

Last weekend my husband and I were visiting friends on the
coast and I decided to hike up a mountain near their cabin.
Once I'd reached the top I sat on a rock and looked for a long
while at the wild and beautiful ocean, and as I sat there two
images popped into my mind. One was a mental picture of me at
age seven, jumping from one big rock to another on the edge of
the ocean; I could feel the roar of the wind and the surf and my
own joyfulness. The other image that popped into my mind was
from my teenage years. I loved to spend Saturday's at my favorite
place, the library, I read everything I could get my hands on—Sar-
tre, Camus, Tolstoy—and at one point I decided to research what
scientists and other thinkers had written about consciousness so
I could write a paper on the subject for one of my high school
classes. Even at that young age I often thought about suffering,
loss, and grief. A boy in my 9th grade class committed suicide and
my closest friend in high school had a breakdown, attempted suicide, and disappeared from my life into a psychiatric institution.

My friends and I weren't very mature emotionally yet but we were investigating all kinds of very heavy adult intellectual ideas. It was a very heady time for me. I could see there was a world out there that I wanted to explore. My mother was nervous about my behavior. I think the kind of person I was becoming and the things I'd taken an interest in perplexed her. I was not one of the teenage girls trying to figure out what color nail polish to put on. My family didn't have a clue about my interests and my friends. At the time the careers open to women were limited to being a nurse, a teacher, or a secretary, but things were changing, values and lifestyles were being questioned, and I knew that I wanted to think differently from the way my parents did. My father was a business man and thought mainly about his daily work, and my mother just worried and wondered what was going on in my head. I know what it's like to think about the darkness of life and experience some of that darkness. I did it through literature during my teenage years. Now that I think back on those days I guess I was a rather scary 16 year old.

Though I was aware at a young age that happiness was the primary goal of life for many, I had no interest in embracing a happy, carefree life. My parents wanted me to marry a doctor whose family had a summer home and a sailboat. When I was 21 years old I married a factory worker's son. We were both in college, he was studying English and theater; I was in psychology. We had no money and no plans, and then everything changed for us. It in the fall of 1969, America was at war in Vietnam and my husband, John, got a very low draft number. We strongly objected to the war; my husband wouldn't even consider going into the service. It was a year of student strikes and demonstrations all over the country. John and I were graduating that spring, and my parents were horrified when we joined a large group of students in protesting the war by wearing white armbands over our robes at graduation. In fact, my parents and many others walked out of the commencement ceremony. That slim armband carried huge symbolic weight for both our cohort and theirs. It was a very difficult time.

My husband's plan was to teach English, but when draft deferments for teachers were revoked, we had three choices—Canada, jail, or enrolling in a seminary where students were eligible for deferment. At the time many Protestant seminaries were playing a role in the sanctuary movement. John registered at a Methodist seminary and began studying for the ministry. I found a job as a secretary.

Then another unexpected opportunity presented itself. A former professor of mine who had been working with the local school board for years to get a psychology course into high schools was given the OK on a trial basis. He asked me if I wanted to teach it. I was 22. I had never taught a class of anything in my life. Now I was teaching a class at the high school level on a subject so new that there weren't any textbooks available for that age group. I had to make up the course out of whole cloth while relying on more advanced texts for reference. Everything kind of fell into it—I guess that's how life happens. You have to be open to these happy surprises and grab them. That was my first year of teaching and I've been a teacher ever since.

You have to be open to these happy surprises and grab them.

During his time at seminary, my husband took an internship year with a small church and I went back to school to get a master's degree in psychology. I completed my M.A. degree (my husband still had two years of seminary left) and took a part-time job teaching at a community college and a second part-time job at a department store selling dresses. Later the community college offered me a full-time job teaching.

When John was nearing graduation, he had walked into the seminary office one day to inquire what the procedure was to get listed for jobs. As he was waiting for the person talking on the phone to finish her conversation, she looked up at him and said to whomever she was talking with, "Hold on, I think I've just found the perfect person for the job." That's how my husband became the youth director at an enormous, wealthy, suburban Congregational church.

He liked the work there and hoped to get hired on for the following year, but both the senior pastor and the associate minister resigned unexpectedly just as that year ended, and John was asked to take over the leadership of the church. He became their senior pastor at age 25, we left our two-room student apartment and moved into the four bedroom parsonage.

Then my life then began changing as fast as his.

I gave up my job at the community college and decided that if I was ever going to move ahead in my field I needed a Ph.D. I explored various possibilities was eventually offered a full scholarship for which I will be forever grateful, because we would never have been able pay the tuition ourselves. The focus of my studies was psychology and religion. My son was born while I was working on my degree but I managed to keep up with my studies. John's job kept him very busy, I gave birth to a second child, a daughter, and our lives were filled with responsibilities and activity. My husband loved his job, I was enjoying my studies, and we had a good life. Then we had another decision to consider. The neighborhood we lived in and the congregation that my husband served was upper class. We felt our children wouldn't fit into the schools and a neighborhood where the kids went off to ski in Switzerland over winter break. We wanted to move to a place where there was more socio-economic diversity. It was time for another change.

John was offered a job as senior minister of a Congregational church in a smaller city in the Midwest. I finished my dissertation, graduated and received my Ph.D. degree at the university in our new location. I had no clue as to what I would do after I earned my degree; I had no plan or specific goal. I decided to wait until something looked appealing but soon learned that the university where I'd just received my doctorate was looking for someone to teach a course on aging, dying and death.

They hired me for a year. I knew then that I loved teaching and the academic life and wanted it to be my lifetime profession. After that year I was hired as an assistant professor. I knew they really wanted me when they wrote a job description to fit my specific education, skills, and experience. They didn't open the position for applications but offered it directly to me. I was in my 30's. We were settled down permanently. Each of us had jobs we enjoyed, our kids got along fine in school, we liked the city, the people, the neighborhood, and we very much enjoyed the life we had.

I'm still at the same university and now I'm a full professor with tenure. My work is still challenging, interesting and, I believe, important. When I was on my sabbatical year I interviewed people in their homes who were dealing with early dementia. They were still active in their communities. I also attended some memory support groups. People with early dementia should be able to volunteer in jobs and activities that don't require less responsibility but keep them engaged in the workplace and socially active. People need to feel like their lives have meaning.

I also spent half of my sabbatical year running creative engagement programs with people in our county nursing homes who have advanced dementia and have lost their language skills. We did painting, storytelling, and song. At the end of the year I considered writing an academic book about my experience, but chose instead to produce a work with wider appeal. My husband is collaborating with me on it. We've just given draft copies of the first three chapters to a random group of people in our community to get their reactions. We want the book to be helpful, useful, and available to a broad population.

Some people live in that dark world of forgetfulness for a good part of their later life, and I believe it's my calling to reach out to those people.

We're including a number of stories in the book because personal experience is often the best way to convey ideas and advance suggestions for meaningful engagement with the community. The book is about the progressive forgetfulness and memory loss that so often happens in later life, but it's also about friendship and community. Some people live in that dark world of forgetfulness for a good part of their later life, and I believe it's my calling to reach out to those people.

Although the book is still in progress, I want to give you a further update on Susan and John's life. Both children have finished their education and are out on their own, and now, as people in mid-life often do, Susan and John have begun reordering their priorities. John decided to leave the church where

he had been minister for 23 years. The congregation was strong and he felt if he was ever going to do something different he should make the change while he had energy to begin again. They discussed what was most meaningful to each of them at this time of their lives. For Susan it was continued learning and teaching; for John it was a life of service. He accepted a job as the workplace chaplain with Good Will, serving people who were chronically ill, ex-prisoners, and developmentally disabled. "I've spent many years telling people to be generous and care about and serve the poor and needy. Now it's my time to do the same," he explained. Although the new position comes with a much decreased income, they have made adjustments with the same flexibility that has been their life pattern.

We no longer have expenses related to the needs of the children, I have good health insurance and my husband is on my plan. I'll continue to work for as long as I can teach, relate to my students and watch them grow, and do my writing and research. I love my job. I'm excited about generating ideas and sharing them with others. Our mortgage payment is manageable, we don't have debts or big expenses, and neither of us have many needs. We're certainly not talking about deprivation; it's more about adding to our lives the time and space for the things that are fulfilling to us. I've started to do my clothing shopping in my closet. There's plenty there. I really don't need anything and in reality there's nothing that I want. This shirt I have on today I bought 15 years ago. I don't wear it often but I still like it. We don't need stuff, we don't need things. We have what we need. We're very blessed so we deliberately reconfigured our life to enable us to do meaningful work and serve others.

One of the biggest drawbacks to our new economic situation is that we can't give as much money away as we used to. That probably sounds paradoxical but we've always been committed to giving 10% of our total income away; now that's a whole lot less than it was before.

One of the wonderful and satisfying things that has changed in our lives is our social schedule. During his 30 years of church ministry John worked weekends. Now we have them open and we can invite friends over. It's so good to be able to share a meal, have people come and stay over the weekend and just share in that way.

We also enjoy an occasional weekend getaway to a tiny cabin we bought on lake a few hour's drive from the city. We kayak and hike in the summer and go snow-shoeing in the winter. I love it best in the winter when the snow is five feet high. I enjoy camping and sleeping in a tent. When I'm in nature I'm a very happy person.

The future is likely to have some stressful and painful events in store as well, but I think that aging can help a person get a realistic acceptance of such things. Many people deny their aging, they hide from it. I guess I've always had a fairly mature view of life because I've been willing to open the book of life to the dark pages.

Now I'm in my 60's. My aging is bringing me to the end of my own life, and I think about those losses in my early days. I think too about my mother who is frail and failing. Her birthday is a few months away. The other day I saw a birthday card that was just perfect for her. I bought the card but she may not still be here on her birthday. At this time of my life I really know that every day is a blessing. We never know when life may be taken away. I look at my husband during an evening when he's playing the guitar and I'm reading and I think, "I must keep this moment." It's ordinary time but I invest in it and give it meaning. As I lie next to my husband in bed, I touch his skin and think, "I must remember this."

I believe in a God of love that suffers with us, and I imagine that I will find consolation in that belief when I need it. My world view includes a sense of how humans can connect with the sacred. I define myself as an "edgy Christian"; who I am has a lot to do with Christianity. I was raised in a Presbyterian church and spent all of those years with John in the Congregational church. But I call my belief "edgy" because I ask a lot of questions. I'm not orthodox in any way. I continue to explore how a person can live their best life guided by religious values, yet all of my values aren't religious based. I'm very open to studying other religions and seeing how they might help me get a fuller, deeper sense of the sacred. A friend of mine is a Jewish woman rabbi and so much of what I've learned from her has become important to me. Theologically I want to go deeper. There are core questions that I want to keep exploring; what does forgiveness mean? What does sin mean? What is holiness and how does it connect with the everyday? What does it mean to receive and give a blessing? How can a particular religious tradition give shape to such questions and help me to understand who I am, how I'm living, and want to live?

I believe in a God of love that suffers with us, and I imagine that I will find consolation in that belief when I need it.

As I look back from my current position as a tenured professor at a university campus that offers me an opportunity to teach and write, do research and earn a decent salary as well, I realize how lucky I am, and yet I don't know how much longer I'm going to want to devote myself to a full-time job. I sometimes find myself thinking about what I might explore in the years ahead with less time constraints. I have a lot of energy and several areas of experience I'd still like to explore, but I know I have my limits. My university job is full time, John and I are working on writing our book, and I like to take time to visit my son and daughter; I'll have a grandchild soon. They live more than six hours away but close to each other so I see them both when I take time off to spend a few days with them.

I'm looking forward to experiencing time in a different way as I grow older. Though my life is full and rich, it's often over-scheduled right now, and I'm always asking what time it is or looking my watch or a clock. I'd like to experience time a little differently, remaining open to and relishing the unexpected. As I grow older, I want to work on being quiet and still. I want to develop the spiritual discipline of minding the moment. It might not be easy. Yet I relish the spiritual challenge of un-learning my attachment to time and divesting myself of the need for measurable accomplishment in the eyes of others.

Several years ago I wrote a book with a colleague that we titled, *Aging and the Meaning of Time*. I'm beginning to think we could better have called the book, *Time and the Meaning of Aging*. I'm excited about my aging; I think there are new discoveries to be made.

> **To exist is to change, to change is to mature,**
> **to mature is to go on creating oneself endlessly.**
> – Henri Bergson

AFTERTHOUGHTS

The choice of work, service, and lifestyle that Susan and her husband have voluntarily chosen is not the usual pattern in American life. Their voluntary simplicity isn't a drastic change for them but reflects a consistency in life style and priorities that have been primary in their lives. Growing numbers have harkened to the call to pull back from the seductions of consumer culture—some by necessity, others by choice. Seeds of Simplicity and Simple Living America are two organizations that have captured the interest of individuals throughout the country seeking to find fulfillment and passion in ways not related to buying, spending and accumulation.

I once collected a series of interviews with persons who volunteered at hospitals, nursery schools, summer camps, and other service institutions to be found in most communities. The overwhelming response I got from those volunteers was, "I get back far more than I give." Susan and John have shaped their retirement plans around service to others; In addition to the people they serve, their story can open our eyes to the satisfactions of devoting ourselves to meaningful activity. Sometimes all we need is a role model to inspire and motivate us.

Susan's story from her early years through the present has a rare continuity. Who she is now is a mature version of who she has always been. Her flexibility in dealing with changing circumstances and the depth of her values from her early years reflect a story of creating oneself endlessly. Susan actually has expressed excitement about her aging and welcomes this new time of her life. She seems to be forever the teacher and the student as well; a great example of how we might welcome our own aging and learn by making aging our partner.

Jeanette (age 75)

"Only when your consciousness is totally focused on the moment you are in can you receive any gift, lesson, or delight that moment has to offer."

– Barbara De Angelis

Jeanette greeted me at the door of her home with a warm embrace. Before I had finished setting up my equipment to record our interview she began talking, "There's a surprising joy in being who I am now at the age of 75," she said with a smile. "Certainly I had pleasure and moments of happiness in my younger years, but I continue to marvel at the presence of the underlying joy I'm feeling now."

Stories of her past would have to wait. It was obvious that Jeanette wanted to start our conversation with who she was today. We began, and Jeanette spoke again about joy.

I've never been this joyful. It isn't that something has come into my life that makes me joyful; my joy comes from within. It's a joy that I never felt when I was younger. I was overlaid with guilt, with burdens and religious teachings that told me I was a sinner. I've spent much of my life listening to a judgmental voice that whispered in my ear, "Who do you think you are anyhow?"

I struggled to try to be perfect. I never had a sense of the richness that I am as a person. I really like myself now.

Jeanette fell silent as she gazed at the beauty of her garden and the vast field of grasses and wild plants that surround her small home. Peacefulness and calm radiated from her. She seated herself in a nearby chair and began reflecting.

The three words that describe my life at this time are gentleness, pleasure, and ease. I enjoy certain pleasures: walks, butterflies, rain drops. It's easy. Why do I have to make life hard for myself? I've spent many years working to make the world a better place. My life has been a life of giving back in many ways. I worked in the jail system, ran my husband's foundation, and gave money to individuals and groups to seed their dreams of creating a small business. Another time in my life I was a model and had a television show. Now I'm trying a different way of living my life. I'm doing that by just being who I am. I'm just into loving what I live each moment.

I live pretty simply. It's a very different life than when I lived in a large city. Now I live in a rural planned community that is wild, woody, and ecologically conscious. My house is small and manageable. I live in contentment with my three cats. I'm only 90 minutes out of the large city I used to live in, so I can take a train or drive in any time I feel a need for a big-city fix. The few days a month that I go into the city are at a very different pace. People are talking and doing and planning and looking at their watches so they don't miss a train or an appointment. At one time that was my life as well. Now I live very differently here in the country. I've chosen to live these later years quietly and with a good deal of solitude. I can calm the chatter in my mind, tune into the sounds of nature, and enjoy the sacredness of silence.

I was raised a right-wing fundamentalist: don't drink, don't smoke, don't play cards, don't go with the boys that do. I had to wear my hair a certain way, always be modestly dressed—my younger life was pretty joyless. I've spent much of my life trying to heal from that. I've run away from organized religion. I don't consider myself religious in the institutional sense. There were wise prophets in every religion . . . Buddha . . . Jesus. Yet, in my opinion the followers rigidified their message into an organizational, doctrinal form. For me this takes away the spirit of religion. I call myself "post-Christian." I do have deep beliefs. Let's just say that in my life, now, everything is holy, everything is sacred.

When I was in the stage of life that we now label mid-life, I thought I had come so far, grown so much in experience, that I was certain I had achieved balance and even wisdom. I know now that I still had far to grow. How could I know anything about what it was like to be 75 from my perspective at 55? I worked hard figuring out who I was in my 50s. Now I'm figuring out who I am at 75. My way of living is a relatively new stage of acceptance in my life.

There were times in my life when I was extremely busy and lived by a daily list of things I had to do. If you had asked me then what would be the priorities in my life now I never could have answered. My story has many layers.

My first marriage lasted 16 years. I was very young when we married. My first husband was a rigid religious conservative. We struggled with intimacy, both of us damaged by our histories and the chains of a strict and loveless religion. Finally I realized I had to get out of the relationship or it would literally kill me. The divorce took several years and was messy and mean. But at last I was free.

At the time we divorced, my husband took all of the money that we had laboriously saved together and put into a business venture. He lost the money within a year and a half and never had another job. Even now, he's on welfare. So I became a single mom with two children. I had to work to financially support us. I was always multi-tasking to get through the day—raising the children, working full time, taking care of everything. I barely had time to wash my hair! Later, when the children were older, I went back to school to get an advanced degree and train for a career.

My second husband was handsome and rich. He had five children and close family connections. Through him I learned to enjoy the pleasures of this beautiful world, something that was missing from my earlier life with so much emphasis on sin. We traveled, partied, read poetry, and drank good scotch in the evenings. It was fun. We spent summers on an island of incredible beauty in Canada with our children and many of their friends. We sailed, fished, swam in the setting sunlit waters. It was the life I needed to release my up-tightness and open my eyes to a bigger world.

Gradually I became aware that my husband was drinking too much. I was drinking too much as well. It was a dangerous influence on the teenage children in our lives; this was the shadow side of our pleasures. The alcohol was taking over our lives. I was no longer feeling liberated, but in a new type of bondage. Through Al-Anon, I learned that I was codependent and an enabler.

We had some harsh fights over what was happening, and I struggled with desperation and depression. Even thinking of another divorce was devastating. Broken dreams are, for me, the most horrible pain. I cried and swung between hating myself and hating him. My husband refused to see his drinking as a problem in the family. To my dismay, he chose to stay in his old patterns. He divorced me. It was a dark time for me and my children. I will be forever grateful to his children for being a part of my life and helping me heal from the pain of my first marriage. This was a new chapter in my life. I gained a depth of experience and lost the burden of naiveté.

The alcohol was taking over our lives. I was no longer feeling liberated, but in a new type of bondage. Through Al-Anon, I learned that I was co-dependent and an enabler.

My third marriage lasted 13 years, until my husband's death. His illness taught me something about death and dying. I wanted him to handle his illness a certain way, my way—to talk about his feelings, fears, all of that. But he didn't want to talk about it. He wanted to believe that everything was going to be all right. I couldn't share with him that I knew that his time was getting shorter and shorter. He had an ability to pretend that things were going to be fine. If I loved him I had to do his illness and death his way. I finally realized that I had to go to friends to have someone to talk with about my feelings and fears.

One time I left my husband in the care of others and went away alone for a couple of days. A friend had offered me her house, as she was out of town. On the second day I was there I remember a wave of grief took hold of me. I cried and yelled and screamed loud and long. I guess I had given myself permission to do this, and I did it again at other times when I was alone and in a safe place. I was so grateful for my friends. I felt deep grief many times during my husband's long illness. It was the heaviness of his suffering during the very long period of his illness that was the most grief-producing thing for me. I've learned to handle grief by letting it have its way. When my husband died, his children were there, hospice was there. I had what I needed to begin healing.

During her husband's long illness, Jeanette had thoughts and plans about possible work and areas of interest she might pursue in the future. We all know how the most carefully made plans often are overthrown by circumstances beyond our control. So many times I've heard people say, "Life is what happens while you're making other plans." So it was with Jeanette's plans for the new career she had anticipated.

Her husband's will provided for creating a foundation that would continue the philanthropic work he had championed during his life. For many years he had provided financial assistance to people in developing countries. His generosity was aimed at helping people to help themselves. The plan was to give grants or loans to people who had practical dreams of creating small, community-based businesses. Much of the money went to women to help them get out of poverty, to help make their dreams of independence come true. The terms of Jeanette's husband's will designated that his wife was to serve as the foundation's key administrator for the entire time of its existence. The foundation was funded for a period of ten years.

It was a new career for me and one I didn't choose. It chose me. It took me a year to learn my job. I knew it was a privilege to serve others, and the experience helped me grow into a world I really didn't know before. My most important learning was about compassion and caring. It was a gift to me to be involved in that process; it was a joy to contribute to helping so many. We had ten years to distribute the money, and then the foundation was depleted as planned. During the final year of the foundation I prepared to resume a life of writing and explore the many other interests I wanted to pursue.

I was 68 and financially comfortable. There were many things that interested me personally. One was patterns of personal growth and change as we age. My first undertaking was to write a book entitled *What Are You Doing With The Rest of Your Life*. My next project was to create a radio talk show that focused on the subject of aging.

I poured my energy and determination into building a mid-life career. Then one of those things that can change your life in an instant happened to me. I was diagnosed with colorectal cancer. It was a terrible, disorienting shock.

I started chemotherapy and radiation. Surgery would be the next step if my doctor felt it was indicated. When disease entered my life, the first thing that flashed through my mind was, "What am I to learn from this?" I spent time in meditation and did considerable thinking about what meaning this tumor would have in my life. I had a deep sense that I had something vitally important to learn from this experience.

I began to think that the cancer inside me was there to teach me something about my relationship with my son. He was very sick from cocaine and heroin; his marriage had ended in divorce, and he was in prison twice for drug-related offenses. I had spent enormous time and energy feeling that his problems were my fault for not having been a better mother. I had made many efforts to get my son in treatment for his drug addiction. There was an arrogance inside of me that knew exactly what the best recovery treatment for him was, how he should live—that my plan for fighting his addiction was the right plan. I acted as if it was my responsibility to fix him. I was trying to manage his addiction and cure.

I came to feel that the cancer inside me was there to teach me that the only life I could save was my own. It wasn't my job to save him. In the quiet of my mind I began getting messages to stop all the many efforts that I had pursued for my son that had failed to cure his drug addiction. I started to see that I was constantly trying to control decisions in the lives of others. Was it a wake-up call? As I looked at my behavior with more honesty I knew I had to find a way to let go of my regrets and move on.

> *I started to see that I was constantly trying to control decisions in the lives of others.*

I'm happy to tell you that now, in my later years, I've finally learned how to give up trying to tell my adult children how to live their lives. They are all in mid-life now. I watch their lives unfold, but I don't interfere. We now are able to have pleasant phone conversations and good visits when we plan them together, and I'm free to be me. I hope my children will remember that I got out there and worked and supported them when their father left us with nothing, and that even if I made mistakes I was always there for them, that I never abandoned them, and that I really love them.

As my cancer treatments continued, I withdrew and spent many months in quiet meditation and prayer. I connected in my own way to God, the Divine, The Great Other. I read poetry where I found wise and inspirational words, and I would only see people who made me feel better, never those that drained my energy. When pain came I learned to listen to it, and somehow then it didn't hurt so much. Sometimes when I was in pain, I'd look out my window and see a butterfly or a plant in bloom or something that I felt was saying, "Don't give up." I lived my process fully, and the veil between this world and whatever that other world is became so very thin for me.

After Jeanette's radiation and chemotherapy treatments, her doctor took many scans and did many tests. Surprisingly, it appeared that the tumor had disappeared. To be safe, the doctor scheduled her for surgery, even though the tests no longer indicated it was necessary. He warned her that if even one cell was left the cancer might return. After deep introspection, Jeanette decided not to have the surgery.

At my two-year check-up my doctor said, "Jeanette, you're my favorite patient because you proved me wrong." The cancer was a major transforming experience in my life. I became more patient, slowed the pace of my life, and stopped judging other people— and myself. I was able to let all that go. Out of that experience I found a new acceptance of life. I don't have bad days anymore; I don't even have bad moments. I've become what I never believed I'd be: a contented and happy person. Things are much different at this time of my life than I ever would have imagined.

I learned from this experience that I don't have to live my life to please people—not my son, my daughter, anyone. I knew I needed to cut down the noise in my life. I embraced solitude; I thrived on silence. My feelings changed from loneliness to joy in being alone, by connecting with a home place inside of me that all of my life I had been looking for. This has become the best season of my life in many ways. Sure, my physical self is diminishing. I can't hike mountains or ski anymore. I don't stay up late.

And there are other activities I just can't do or don't wish to do anymore. Yet there are many things growing in the face of this diminishment: my sense of myself, deep feelings of love, and my awareness of losing my judgmental nature.

My life has turned into the honoring of the ordinary, the small things. I see the world differently. One day I was in my garden and swept away a little pile of ant houses because I didn't want their piles of sand on my patio. As I was doing that, I remembered a line from a poem I had read recently. "What kind of a god would we have if he did not hear the bangles on the ants ring as they move the earth in their sweet dance?" If there are bangles on ants and God notices, I thought, I'd better pay attention. So early the next morning I got down on my knees and looked at the small, neat piles of sand the ants had built overnight. As I watched, an ant dropped a piece of sand on the top of the pile, then bounced back down the hole he'd come out of. Another ant dropped his sand right at the edge of the pile. It was amazing to watch. The ants were a community, working together to build something. Who was I to sweep their accomplishment away? This experience inspired me to write a poem that I call "A World Beneath Mine."

Neat circles of sand appear overnight on my brick patio,
each centered where two bricks meet.
I don't like this . . . all those ants under my patio.

How many summers, have I tried to discourage them,
swept their circles away,
sprayed bug killer down the center.
You see, eventually, my bricks sink.

Then one day as I remembered the ancient words of the poet Hafiz I came upon this thought: "And what kind of a God would he be if he did not hear the bangles ring on an ant's wrist as they moved the earth in their sweet dance? . . .What a God, what a God we have!"

This thought inspired me to write the following verses.

Next morning at dawn, when all is touched with hope,
I sit beside a new sand circle and watch.
Each ant carries its burden up and out, placing the grain
where it chooses. Some prance
with their load, some struggle barely making it.

For once, I admire their work.
Like an intricate sand painting, the beauty is fleeting.
But in this moment I praise what once I ignored.

So I'm beginning to notice little things, little miraculous things. And I'm beginning to think that maybe they aren't small things, maybe they're big things. This kind of thinking has become part of my daily life. Poetry is only one my creative activities these days.

When I was younger and would hear the word "creativity," I would think of a large beautiful mural on a wall or a book that's on the *New York Times* bestseller list. Now I have a different understanding of creativity. I think of creativity as energy that I want to live in every day, in the smallest of my tasks. Small things in my life require creative energy. I use creative energy when I find just the right pot to transplant this plant on my table. Even preparing a simple meal, that's creative energy. I do things that others might consider creative, like doing sketches and writing poetry, but I see creativity as a larger energy than an accepted art form. Creativity is the energy that flows through everything I do throughout the day. Everybody has that kind of creativity.

I write a lot now—poetry, journal writing—and I'm contemplating writing another book from the point of view of these later years of my life. When I embrace the challenge of writing, there's an enthusiasm that comes to me. But also when I read poetry there's an energy that comes up inside me. Hearing the words and touching the feelings of others through their words nourishes my soul and comforts my heart. There are words that are like a pillow that you can lay your head upon and find comfort. And there are other words that offer a creative challenge for my mind to think differently and for my spirit to expand.

I believe that older persons can become empowered to speak out against social injustice, to stand for fairness and mercy. We can open in our later years to a kind of generativity. We can give gifts, not material things, but gifts of self that last beyond our lifetime. We have more leverage and know-how than when we were young. We can take less compromised stands than the young, speaking honestly in ways both in small and big.

We can model deeper, more rewarding relationships, where compassion, playfulness, and respect for differences are the norm.

We can model deeper, more rewarding relationships, where compassion, playfulness, and respect for differences are the norm. We can form new definitions of beauty, strength and creativity. We can contribute to building a better world. And when we reach the end of our lives, we can let go, embracing the mystery of what comes next because we have learned to trust life, to risk, to love, to really live.

For most of my life I defined myself as a seeker. Now I'm a finder. At 75 I have found a home place inside me, a place that always was there but was covered over. It was covered over by all the responsibilities I had: the anger, the ambition, the demands of being who I wanted to be. So much has been stripped away—all those things I thought I needed to be happy: a husband, youthfulness.

Now, here I am with wrinkles all over my face and hips that are wider than I hoped they would be, and still I am happy. I'm so happy that I don't know how to express it to people. There's nothing on the outside that makes me happy; it just rises up inside me. I look at a beautiful blue sky, and the clouds and the sun are kissing all those clouds. It's exquisite, and it's become a priority for me to appreciate the gifts that are all around me every moment. This is what I have if I live in the moment, each moment as it comes. I'm so grateful that I can see everything simply and in the moment.

How did I get to this place? I think it was Gandhi who said that you should never give up anything unless what you want in its place is worth more to you than what you're giving up. I've found it easy to give up wanting to look younger or finding a lover or other things I had once wanted, because I've found something I want more. I now have freedom from the values I lived with in the past, and I've chosen to explore what it is to be a wise old woman.

Maybe there's another way of saying this than "giving up." Maybe "letting go" says it better. I've let go a lot of furniture that I had to polish and dust. I gotten rid of memorabilia I've been holding on to. I've given many boxes of books to the library. I've let go of things, things that formerly were so important to me. I want space. I want discretionary time. I want fewer things to take care of. I want simplicity, not stuff. I want to enjoy the ordinary day and the things in an ordinary day.

I don't mean to sound like I never have doubts or that I don't sometimes slip and catch myself falling into my old self. Just a few days ago I went to a concert. I had a seat on the aisle, and as people walked past me to their seats I made judgments: that woman's dress is too tight, that one is too fat, that one is too thin. I caught myself, realized that my old pattern had surfaced, and let it go. What good does this kind of thinking do for my life, my immune system? What good does it do to others to put out negative messages? Things like this happen less and less in my life, I'm happy to tell you.

What I've come to trust is that I'm in a process of transition. Yet I have a profound sense that there is some kind of grace, energy, some kind of a knowingness that will push me or kick me or open me or carry me to the next step. I might resist, I might not understand it at the time, but for now my only concern is how I am going to enjoy the day and each experience the day brings.

In the first half of life I went out to discover who I was in this funny, silly, dark, frustrating world. Then came the unease of my middle years. And then came an opportunity—no, it's more than this—to go inward. I know that now is my time to simplify and listen to my still small voice within, the deepest part of myself. And that's what I would tell others, because it's available to all of us.

We old are beautiful. Certainly a handsome, energetic young person is beautiful, too, but that kind of beauty fades in time. It's going to go, and then we have the opportunity to develop another beauty. The paradox is that I look in the mirror at an old wrinkled woman, but inside I feel beautiful, I feel loving. I now know how to love.

There are pieces of my conversation with Jeanette that were exchanged over lunch or our afternoon tea and never recorded.

I can't share with you Jeanette's exact words, but I can share her thoughts. She quoted a poem by Mary Oliver entitled *The Journey*. It began like this: "*One day I finally knew what I had to do ….*" She recited the closing line with passion and resolve: "*. . . determined to do the only thing you could do, determined to save the only life that you could save.*" I recall that one critic said this poem captures the very moment that you take your heart in your hands and walk into a new life.

By accepting my losses and aligning with what I believe at this time of my life are life's deeper truths, I feel a freedom to live in harmony with what has heart and meaning for me. I believe I will continue to grow because my future self is courting me today.

The future belongs to those who live intensely in the present.

– Anonymous

AFTERTHOUGHTS

To experience Jeanette's calm, her radiant joy, her comfort with taking each day as it came, was very special for me. Her message was just what I needed to hear: slow down, simplify your life, invite into your days different ways of seeing and being. I hope her message speaks to you as well.

One last thought: The people I interview often talk about taking the time to watch a flower open, to simply sit by a lake and savor the calm, to meditate and just be rather than do. I truly believe that when the outer world shrinks, the inner world can grow. Jeanette's story illustrates this gift of aging.

Jenny (age 52)

I plunged into the job of creating something from nothing....
I considered cash money as the smallest part of my resources
...I had faith in a living God, faith in myself, and a desire
to serve.

— Mary McLeod Bethune

Every 10 seconds someone in the United States turns 50. Many still look at that turning point as a mid-life crisis, a negative thing, not as an opportunity to embrace in a new way their maturing insights about the world and themselves. Maybe Jenny's story of what she's doing and feeling at this time of her life will inspire others to seek and explore their own path of meaning and purpose in the second half of their lives. Here is her story.

I'm 52 years old now. I used to work as a senior high English teacher of advanced composition and literature, and I loved my job. My husband's work involved a good deal of travel, and when my children were five months and three years old, I made the decision to stay home and take care of them. When the children were bigger I went back to teaching and once again, I really enjoyed it and was very happy doing that work. My life is very different now.

Everything changed for me when three of my friends had surgery for breast cancer. There was one particular experience that changed the direction of my life. I went with a friend to look at wigs after she had lost her hair due to chemotherapy. The person who waited on us was impatient and showed no interest in my friend as an individual going through a difficult time of her life. It was a very rushed sales pitch without any empathy or sympathy. The salesperson merely recited the prices and information in a routine manner and kept looking at her watch. My friend was devastated by the cold, impersonal experience. She had gone through a double mastectomy and was very self-conscious and fragile. I watched the entire scene feeling angry and helpless.

I couldn't easily forget my friend's discomfort that day, and during a drive with my husband not long afterward I complained to him at some length about the inhumane treatment she had experienced. That evening I was still grumbling to him and he loudly said to me, "So do something about it!"

And I did. My new business was incorporated the following week. That was the birth of Lily Wellness Inc, a one-stop shop for wigs, caps, hats, and other items for women cancer patients who are getting either chemotherapy or radiation therapy treatments. I wanted it to be a place of privacy, personal comfort and support. I know that my reasons for starting a business were different from why most people go into business. I was following my emotions. It was an epiphany of sorts, I guess. It came from within, from my religious beliefs and my feelings of wanting to be available to those I could help. I think it was a new awareness at this time of life, a mid-life coming together of my religious faith, my profession and certainly my personal life.

My husband and I borrowed money from the bank and

put some of our savings into the business as well. How ironic, I thought, my friends are thinking of retirement and I'm starting a business. My husband said as long as I could pay my bills and feel good about what I was doing, he'd put up with my hours away from home and even help me set up my shop. My friends saved up coupons so I could buy my lamps and shelves and things at a discount. I've had office furniture donated and I've gotten a very affordable rent from the people who own this building. I had a lot of support. My store is a one stop shop, I personally do all of it; fitting breast prostheses, bras, swimwear. I fit and order the custom wigs, and I stock hats, turbans, scarves, T-shirts, skin-care preparations, journals and books. I also sell prayer shawls that I knit myself. It's a very personal business.

When I come to work early in the morning I never know what my day is going to be like, what the mood of the next person coming in will be, or what specific kind of support they will be looking for. Sometimes people cry. I've cried too with some women. I've also laughed a lot. And there's usually a mutual hug on the way out, even if we've only met an hour before. These are great women. They trust me, I trust them. Every woman that comes in has her own story and their own way of handling their situation. I'm open to listening to it all. Every woman is different from the one that just walked out the door or the one that will be here when this one leaves.

Every woman that comes in has her own story and their own way of handling their situation. I'm open to listening to it all.

Some really great women come into my store; young mothers who are in chemotherapy who are rushed and harried; they've had to get sitters for the appointment and they have enormous family responsibilities besides dealing with their cancer recovery treatments. When they get comfortable with me and more comfortable with the process of fitting a wig they bring their young children with them. I have toys and games and other things to keep young ones busy. One client had both her grandma and granddaughter in with her and they all left with matching hats.

One of my clients is a ninety year old woman who had one breast removed. The remaining breast was beginning to sag—almost to her waist. She had not been able to wear a bra for 6 months. She was thrilled to be herself again; a new bra gave her a new attitude. No matter how old we are, we have the right to look and feel our very best. It is not vain to want to be the best you can be.

Three sisters came in to celebrate one's birthday and her need for a wig and a hat. They made the experience fun. There were many jokes, much teasing and many tears. They would hug each other when emotions were running high. I was truly honored to be part of something so powerful. The bond between sisters—and between women in general—is a humbling thing. Cancer can't even begin to break down that bond.

A few months ago I was apprehensive before meeting a new client who was only 19 years old. Of course her mother came with her. The thought of having to face such a profound illness with my own daughter shakes me to the core. The fear, pain, and sadness must be overwhelming. Yet the strength this mother and daughter found in each other amazed me. Love and trust were the glue that helped them move forward together.

Humor, too, is a big part of this process. Not loud, boisterous humor but little jokes. I remember one woman who took off her shirt to be fitted for prosthesis. She looks in the mirror at her body and exclaimed, "I always knew I'd end up with one breast looking different than the other one but this is ridiculous!" A new relationship often starts with humor. Some women are very bawdy, others are very prudish; it's how each of us reacts to stress and fear.

I like to stay in touch with my women customers if they make the choice to do so. If they've made it clear they don't want a public association with their wig provider I don't even acknowledge them if I run into them at the mall. Yet a couple of my customers have become new and sincere friends. One woman called this week and offered to bring lunch over and just spend an hour with me. You know, if you take your hair off or if your hair is literally falling out during an appointment here, or you have to show some of your surgery scares to be fitted for anything, you bond pretty quickly.

I really look forward to coming in to work every day. Some days, you know, are very heavy. I go home and I have to de-compress. I have an incredible husband who will be there for me. He has always felt that his job description as a husband includes offering support, and he's always there emotionally for me. He's a great guy.

This work gives me great satisfaction. I meet great women every day, women who are stoic, courageous and inspiring. I have great respect and admiration for these women. I allow a good deal of time for each of my clients—perhaps in that sense I'm not a good business woman, but they need to talk and part of my job is to listen. I'd like to stay in this business as long as I'm healthy. I work hard, long hours and it isn't just the physical work; the emotional work also takes a good deal of energy. As long as I can run this business the way I believe it should be run I'll continue. If I find I'm lacking patience and if I should feel that I'm not giving my clients what they need emotionally and psychologically, then I'll put the business in the hands of someone who understands those needs and has the energy and desire to fulfill them.

I'm getting very busy these days. The need for what I offer and how I offer it isn't going away. There seems to be more and more women diagnosed with breast cancer. I've been looking for someone to act as an assistant who can offer the empathy, sympathy, and support that my clients need. I do have someone in mind that I would like very much to work with. It's actually the woman whose situation inspired me to start this business. I also have past clients that have offered to volunteer. It's clear to me that my future employees will be chosen from among the woman I've helped in the past. They have shown a desire to give back, to help others in the same way I've helped them. I'm proud of that.

Giving is very important to me. That's something my parents instilled in me and my brother and sister at a very young age. The lesson was that you give back in many ways. You give back to the earth, a lesson from the Cherokee Indians, that you leave the earth better than you found it. You help other people, you try to be of service when you can—that was part of my upbringing in the Catholic Church. My brother was just given an award for giving the most pro-bono service of any lawyer in our state. I guess we all learned and have lived that lesson.

You give back to the earth, a lesson from the Cherokee Indians, that you leave the earth better than you found it.

When a new client comes in I'm as friendly and unthreatening as I know how to be. Nevertheless, at some point she might stand up and say something like, "I'm leaving. I can't really do this." One woman started off by saying, "I didn't ever want to come in here and I never wanted to meet you." She broke into tears and I held her and listened.

One woman struck me as rather frivolous on our first encounter. She kept up a rather carefree banter and I judged her as not having much depth. She was overly concerned about how others saw her, I thought to myself, and was working too hard to maintain her composure. Yet as the weeks went on, I found her to be one of the most intelligent, sensitive, courageous women I'd ever dealt with. We've become confidants and friends. Her health has now deteriorated and she has shown enormous courage as a mother and a wife.

That experience taught me not to make snap judgments, but to listen and allow my clients to emerge at their own pace from their public personae. After all, these women are dealing with difficult questions about how to live, and how to face the possibility of their own death in the not-too-distant future. Many of them are sort of like an onion—they slowly unpeel, and my job is to listen with sincerity and sensitivity.

I keep learning every day. But I also do my homework. My first challenge was to learn about various types of female cancer. I had a medical student help me with that. Now I'm exploring various groups that help cancer patients in some way, and working with a group who are investigating legislative options to increase support for cancer patients and their caregivers. I'm pretty far out of my comfort zone with some of this, but it's important that I keep learning so I can serve my clients needs and understand what they're facing.

I don't advertise my business. I believe the way to attract new clients is through the confidence of existing clients. I do believe that newspaper stories and other media stories get the word out that these services are available in a very personal and private way. I contacted a feature writer at our local newspaper and a couple of months after I spoke with him he contacted me and an article was published. That's how you learned about me, and that's how some new clients have come in to see what's available here. Yes, I'm running a business, but because of the relationship I have with the women I think of it more as a service.

I try to keep some balance going in my life so I can exercise, go to the doctor and the dentist, and other appointments. I try to see friends but it's getting harder and harder to find the time, and when I do go out socially, conversation is crippled by the fact that I can't say much about my work because my relationships with the women I serve is confidential. Yet I carry around a lot of emotion about other people's pain and suffering. I do have a garden and that's a blessing for me, a very relaxing experience. I feel the need to talk about my feelings but it isn't ethical to do that, so when I'm out in the garden I talk to the plants and to my dog and the cat. They know how to keep a secret!

I've found an inner strength as I look into the eyes of people who are so tired, so discouraged, and so brave.

I really believe that we have to take care of each other. I have always felt that way. I remember when I was young and learned about the American Indians and I discovered that they always believed that they must take care of each other. They continue to believe that and practice it. I recall that for many years I would tell my mother that I must have some Indian blood in my veins because I too believe that philosophy so strongly.

I've learned a great deal about myself these past months. I have found new strengths, new levels of patience, and a new store of compassion. I've found an inner strength as I look into the eyes of people who are so tired, so discouraged and so brave. I can look at the scars from a mastectomy or brain biopsy and remain calm and professional. I have found my own time of the day to cry for these women. I always make time for prayer and I'm trying to find more time for myself. It's the same advice I always tell family caregivers they must do. I need to take care of myself so I can better care for others. I've found my passion and I'm truly content.

It's important to me to have people think of me as someone who cares about them.

— Diana, Princess of Wales

AFTERTHOUGHTS

People often tell me stories about major life changes they made during their mid-life years in their work, home situation, marriage or lifestyle. It's almost as if a growing sense of maturity or conviction makes such changes easier, or endows them with the compelling force of necessity. Sometimes, as Jenny's story illustrates, an unexpected event will trigger the change. At other times such changes come about after a long period of incubation. Whatever the underlying cause, it seems that dramatic mid-life change is often accompanied by a renewed vitality, energy and a depth of creativity. A person about to tackle a new adventure often burns with a passion and determination that can surprise his or her family and friends. If you, or someone you know, is approaching their middle years with apprehension and anxiety, possibly Jenny's story might change their vision of a mid-life crisis into a mid-life quest. Thirty years ago, when I was approaching 50, it was commonplace to express a negative, despairing attitude about the experience of aging. I'm glad I now live in a time when the middle years are more often considered beginnings than endings.

Ann (age 78)

*Any committee is only as good as the most knowledgeable,
determined and vigorous person on it. There must be
somebody who provides the flame.*

– Lady Bird Johnson

A few months ago I went to a reading by a number of local
writers. One of the authors participating was a tall, older black
gentleman. As he took a seat at the front facing us, I looked
across the room and saw a woman smiling encouragingly at
him. Looking closer, I recognized my classmate Ann from our
freshman English class at the university almost sixty years ago.
She was holding on to her walker and her oxygen tank was
close by. After the program was over we had a happy reunion
and I told her about the interviews I was doing with women of
various ages. "Would you like to include this 78-year-old?" she
inquired. It seemed like a good idea to me. Meet Ann, a woman
who always has her eye on potential change.

I've spend many years being involved in civil and human rights
work and social justice issues, fair housing, and changes in
welfare. Although my physical condition now limits my active
involvement, these are the things I care passionately about, and

I continue to cheer on others who are working toward the same goals, and I offer advice and encouragement, in the hope that openness and acceptance of black persons can keep moving forward. My job now is rather like a watchdog; maybe some don't like my bark but it doesn't keep me from expressing myself.

I learned very early that I was different, and that other kids reacted to that difference. In kindergarten, when we were told to hold hands and make a circle, no one would reach for my hand or touch me. Even at 5 years old I couldn't figure out what was wrong with me when other kids didn't want to include me. A more dramatic incident happened when I was still in grade school. A bunch of kids grabbed my jump rope and said they were going to hang me, lynch me. Perhaps they were reacting to something their par-

I remember my grandmother telling me over and over again that I should be proud of myself, that my family were good people, that they had done the right things in their life even if life was made difficult for them.

ents had said. I can't remember how I got away from them but it made a lasting impression on me. I think it was then and there that knew something was wrong, unjust, unfair and had to be changed. I remember my grandmother telling me over and over again that I should be proud of myself, that my family were good people, that they had done the right things in their life even if life was made difficult for them. I began to realize when I was very young, not only that I was different but that I and other black people were treated differently.

Once I had made this realization, I began to notice other things. There were no black bus drivers in my city, maybe one African American dentist or doctor, and I knew my father couldn't be a member of the local union; though he was an excellent auto mechanic he didn't get paid as well as others who were union members. A couple of my uncles worked in the post office. At that time it was considered the most prestigious and best paying job for a black person. My mom wanted me to be independent; she was a seamstress and hoped I might have greater aspirations. I grew up in an atmosphere of encouragement to be who I was and to do what I wanted to do.

I enrolled in college in the late 1940's, and when I graduated I could see that my path was going to involve making life better for black people in the city and state where I lived. If you were educated and Afro-American you just automatically realized that outside of your personal life there were things you would have to do to encourage or directly involved yourself in making change.

I met my husband when I was an undergraduate at the university. It was winter and he was walking across campus wearing a big fur hat. When I first saw him it looked like he had a live animal on his head! His career has been as a teacher; he was the one of the first black high school teachers in the state. When I became active in local organizations and political groups he gave me a lot of support.

However it wasn't yet my time to be an activist. I was married soon after graduating from college and I took on the role of a young wife, had my four children, and was busy taking care of them and my husband. I didn't really think a lot about my future in terms of what I would do about fairness for black people. Of course I was always aware of prejudice and the lack of fairness to people of my race, but I didn't know much about getting involved in political and social action at that time.

When I felt the time had come for me to start getting involved in something outside of my home, I went through a counselor advisor training program designed for university graduates. At the time I had already had some training in working with adolescents and some course work in social work, and I often attended workshops and special sessions in two different graduate programs. I began working with a broad range of people having problems in the educational system. In many situations I worked with both students and their parents to resolve situations in which the family felt the student had been treated unfairly, or that a teacher had unfairly suspended their son or daughter, and that the school administration wasn't listening to them. I always tried to work out something with the school administration—something less severe than suspension. Many black kids that were suspended would never return to school. I worked to get a less severe punishment for them, rather than risk having them leave school permanently.

Often the principal or the teacher would tell me that the child looked hostile and had behaved aggressively. I quickly discovered that often, when a teacher was reprimanding a student, the child would look away. The teacher would misinterpret this as aggressive or hostile behavior, when in fact that's the way black children often dealt with criticism from their elders—by avoiding looking at the person speaking. It was a common cultural thing with many Afro-American kids.

In time I started to learn about how the Urban League and other organizations worked to correct injustices that black people often met up with—in the area of housing, for example. There were some restrictive housing regulations that prevented black people from purchasing homes or renting in several residential areas. We had friends moving here from other parts of the country and they started to face those restrictions and rejections.

Some of the involvement that Ann has had over the years included being the first chairperson on the city housing committee that held a series of public hearings on the issue of fair housing. The result was the enactment of a fair housing ordinance. She also assisted an Afro-American brotherhood group in resolving conflicts between inmates and staff at the state prison, and she was involved in many protest demonstrations to improve the job climate for African Americans. She also lobbied the state legislature often on behalf of similar causes. Ann was director of community services for her city's branch of the Urban League for many years, served on the board of the local NAACP, and actively supported other efforts for equality and fairness for black persons. She ran for city council once and got 38,000 votes; the white male that won got about 2,000 more. As a result of that campaign, Ann gained greater visibility in her community, which helped in all of her public efforts that followed.

She was excited and supportive of a black student take-over of the state university's administration building in 1969. That was the same campus where she had been a student 15 years earlier.

When that group of black students barricaded themselves in that campus building they knew they were taking a big risk, but they were determined to get an Afro-American Studies Department established at our state university. The African American Action Committee, with encouragement from some professors and others, took over the administration building and staged a sit-in. At that time there weren't any classes in black history, and barely a mention of blacks in American history courses beyond what was required to deal with the issue of slavery. The university made no active effort to attract Afro-American or other minority students. It was an important and powerful action that ended with the creation of an African American Studies Program, while also spurring a special effort on the part of the administration to recruit and retain black students. Many of the students that were leaders of that rebellion have achieved significant careers in universities elsewhere in the country, in government jobs, and other community leadership positions. They were brave folks with a mission. It was a meaningful effort and a lasting accomplishment.

Ann had recently celebrated her 78th birthday. She felt like slowing down a bit and had just retired from the position of vice president of the local branch of the NAACP, along with cutting back on her busy schedule in other ways. These decisions were hers by choice. The next events weren't.

I went to the hospital with pneumonia. My doctor looked at the x-rays and discovered I had lung cancer. It was a shock, although I confess I had been a smoker for many years before giving up the habit about a decade ago. I felt very, very sad when the truth of the diagnosis sunk in. All I could think about was that I wanted to see my children and my grandchildren before I could no longer enjoy them. I had some chemotherapy and I now take daily medications to slow down the growth of the cancer. I've been diagnosed as terminal. When I heard that word I thought that meant I might not live another week. That was several months ago. My last visit to the doctor a week ago indicated no significant change so I'm just carrying on, one day at a time. Sometimes I think that's no different for any of us, one day at a time. None of us know how long we have in this world.

My husband and I have moved out of our family home into a condo in an active living community. I can't go anywhere without my walker, oxygen container and breathing apparatus. My activities are limited now. I still cook and do some simple things around the house, and I'll continue doing them as long as I'm able. I can go out occasionally with help so I'm not totally cut off from the world. We read a lot and we play checkers and other board games, and we watch movies here at home. I even get to the theater and some dance performances once and a while. I don't invite many friends over because I never know when I'm going to run out of energy and need a nap, but I enjoy talking on the phone and keeping up with my friends' activities.

> *They say laughing is good for a person. It's good for me, I know that.*

I have friends that send me cartoons and funny jokes via e-mail. I laugh a lot. They say laughing is good for a person. It's good for me, I know that. I get notes from friends that give me a lot of support and I'm comforted by reading inspirational quotes. I also have my husband who just listens and lets me just talk about things when I'm down or sad or whatever. He's wonderful to do that for me—just listen and be there for me in a loving way. Religion hasn't been something I've turned to for support during this illness; I do occasionally read some religious reading or verse. I have friends that call often, some bring a meal over, others take us places occasionally, and I'm grateful for their warmth, sincerity and friendship.

When I wake up in the morning I check out the weather, think about what I have to do that morning before taking my second rest, read the three newspapers that have been delivered, and think about who I'm going to see or talk with that day. I try to live in the present. Sometimes I write letters to my senators, the mayor or some other elected official about pending legislation. I still feel it's important to express my determination or interest in making things more fair and just. I haven't given up on having my say about issues.

I'm interested in doing what I can to encourage younger people to become leaders. I want them to know what needs to be done, and they have to know too that they can reach for the stars. When I hear about gangs of kids that are violent and destructive, I hope there might be a way to encourage them to turn their energies toward forming gangs for justice. Wouldn't it be wonderful if gangs took an active part in positive acts instead of devoting themselves to dangerous and destructive behavior? The recognition that some of those gang members seek could be gotten from positive actions in place of criminal behavior.

My husband and I have always been interested in change and we still are. I still have intensity about my feelings; yet I no longer can be physically involved in efforts to change things. I'm trying to make the days that I'm still here count to my family and to others in my life. I have a favorite quote that I'd like to share with you. It comes from the writings of the poet, Gwendolyn Brooks.

This is the urgency.
Live and have your
blooming in the whirlwind.

I think that says quite a bit—in fact, it says it all. Live, don't give up, and keep blooming, do your thing in the whirlwind, that's the world. You need to live and make a contribution and give something to the world. I just hope that my life has encouraged others to take action.

I would like to leave behind the idea that people need to think beyond their own personal concerns. I'd like to think that the activities I've been involved in have been part of making our society a better place, a freer place for black people. The job isn't finished and I want young people to know that they can't relax and think because we have a black president the struggle is over. I think racism is so deep in our society that although some gains have been made there are still many struggles ahead. I hope I can leave other Afro-Americans with the desire and a strength to continue to monitor and take action when needed. There's nothing like being involved with others who are committed to the same goals in a struggle. It creates a lasting and beautiful bond. We've built our gains on the shoulders of black activists before us, and I want to do whatever I can to encourage young people to stand on our shoulders and be alert and vigilant. I truly believe that in our lives we really need to work for something beyond ourselves. Such commitments offer a great reward.

> *They have rights who dare defend them.*
> – Roger Baldwin

AFTERTHOUGHTS

For those who have come to see life as a cycle—birth, growth, life, death – dealing with decline and the end of life can retain a focus on living. I recall a conversation I had at one time with a person in their 90's. With comfort and ease the person said, "At my age I'm probably pretty close to death, but death doesn't need my energy right now, life does."

There's much talk these days about find meaning and purpose in our later years. I strongly believe that exploring new interests and defining new meaningful activities are important for many of us in our later years. Yet some carry with them into elderhood the same projects and passions that are part of their very being. People who have put their work and beliefs into seeking a better life for others often find it important to maintain continuity by passing on their passions and convictions to a new generation. Our world of diverse populations is lucky to have persons who can inspire the young to embrace and further their causes, and find new ways to work for fairness and justice.

Pat (age 63)

I met Pat through my work on aging. I had produced a public radio program about family caregivers and was contemplating writing a book. I came across Pat's book on caregivers, and noting that we lived near each other, I made an effort to meet her. From that meeting grew a friendship and an opportunity to share her story of personal growth and change. Pat is eager to talk about who she has become at age 63.

I'm exactly where I need to be in my life now to discover and share my unique gifts. I feel as I grow older that I'm more open, more curious, more willing to learn and take responsibility for my own life. For much of my life I was a victim of those who defined for me who and what I was. Now I've learned to really know and accept myself. I'm able to truthfully say that I'm creating my own life and that I'm in charge. I've learned to take total responsibility for my life. Ironically, there's a lot of freedom in taking on that responsibility.

Before we talked more about who Pat is today, she took a brief look back at who she was.

At one time I had a family life—a husband and a son, who is now an adult. I've been alone now for about 16 years, and I actually love living alone. Not that if an appropriate partner came along I wouldn't be interested, but I have a multitude of contacts and friends, and a full, rich life. I came from a family of eleven children, but our family isn't close. My family sort of left me behind when I married outside of my race and religion, and that has never really healed.

I married at a time when interracial marriage was rather rare. My husband and I had a warm circle of friends that accepted and supported our marriage. However, my marriage was not okay with my family. We were Catholic, but my husband had been married before, and that broke all the rules. My family did love my son. He was so warm and endearing that they accepted him. There's been some reconciliation over the years, but we don't have closeness because there were a number of years when we were out of touch.

I do go to church and I do pray, but for the most part as a way of honoring the divine emerging inside myself and accepting that.

Religion is very important in my life. I grew up in a very Catholic family. I have a sister who's a nun, an aunt who was a nun, a brother who is a priest, and on and on; and I, too, was nun for a while. When I was in my late 40s, things changed dramatically as I felt a need for a deep spiritual life that I wasn't finding within the Catholic Church. It just wasn't there for me. And so I shifted to a more spiritually-based affiliation within the Unity church. It's more focused on finding your spirituality within rather than outside yourself. It's been a real home for me in following a path from the inside out. It's parallel in a way to the core of what I teach in helping people to understand themselves from the inside out—to understand the inside of their body, mind, and spirit, to find their inner direction. I do go to church and I do pray, but for the most part as a way of honoring the divine emerging inside myself and accepting that. I believe there are many ways to honor the divine that lives in everything, and lives through me in who I am and the work I do.

I've known people who say that alienation from their family—because of religious difference, divorce, illness, death—set the stage for major changes in their life. None of those things moved my life into a new direction. My situation was quite different. Several years ago I was kidnapped by a young man who demanded money. I gave him what I had, but he continued to hold me at gunpoint for a number of hours. It was a terrifying experience. I didn't know if my life was going to come to an end. I was able, in spite of my fear, to have some compassion for the young man. We began a conversation that lasted through the hours he held me captive. He talked about his love of art and his ambition. During the whole time he held me at gunpoint, I was so intently occupied trying to be helpful and kind to him that I didn't pay attention to the terror that was building inside my body. He struggled with the idea of releasing me, yet he knew I would call the police. Eventually, he let me go. I remember I was still shaking two or three days after it was over. In the months that followed I was able to put it out of my daily thoughts. What I wasn't aware of was that my body continued to carry the fear and horror of the incident. That was 15 years ago.

As the years passed, I became aware of various aches and pains, stresses and tensions in my body. I sought out a medical diagnosis but my symptoms weren't easily categorized. I was in the habit of pushing myself even if I was fatigued, in pain, or had said yes to more things than I could comfortably take on. Maybe it was about proving I was capable and reliable, but whatever it was, I always pushed myself to the limit of my energy. To seek some relief I decided to register for a workshop on learning to relax tensions and listen to one's body. At the time I was in my 50s.

During the class a chair in the back of the room suddenly fell over and crashed loudly to the floor. It sounded like a gun shot. I started to tremble and shake uncontrollably. I know now that the chair falling was like the gun shot that I had feared might kill me. I tensed and tightened, and the terror came back and multiplied. My body remembered the fear of the robbery incident I had experienced in the past. The residue of the fear, anxiety, and apprehension was stored in my body.

Fortunately the leader of the workshop had great insight. She knew a great deal about listening to the body. She worked quite intensely to get to the other side of the terror that my body was holding onto. She taught me to listen deeply and let the terror pass through. Her skill and wisdom helped me to find a new freedom on the other side. I was astounded by that experience. It was life-giving for me and so revealing about what sits inside our bodies that we don't know is there.

Since that time I've learned and experienced a great deal. I've started to pay attention, delved into meditation, and tried get quiet enough to listen to my body on a deeply emotional and spiritual level. I am convinced that my body—our bodies—are trying to get our attention, but we just don't know how to listen. I was determined to understand how to know my own body and also help others listen to theirs. I became acutely aware of the subject of aging, of changes in my body, along with a strong feeling that I needed to create a new direction in the second half of my life.

One day I was reading a book on mid-life transitions to see what advice it might offer. The author suggested that a person take two years of their regular life and go on a sabbatical, then come back and re-invent their life. That wasn't exactly right for me, because I couldn't quit work for two years and give up the paycheck that I needed to live on. But the idea really appealed to me. So I decided to take my own style of a sabbatical at home.

I cut my commitments down to the minimal work I had to do to sustain an income, which was mostly writing projects for other people, and pretty much eliminated everything else that was nonessential. I dropped all my committee work, my volunteer projects, and all of my social activities. I said to my friends, "I'll call you when I surface, but don't expect to hear from me for a while." I went into seclusion. My life became very quiet. I would sit and look out the window for much of the day and do nothing. This was extremely unusual for me, because I'm a hard worker and a pusher. I somehow was able to just stop. I didn't feel depressed, but I felt a strong need to be quiet and reflective. I decided I was going to do it as long as it took. It was a totally different living rhythm for me, and it was just marvelous. I did that for about four months, and then I started to get just a tiny bit restless.

The author suggested that a person take two years of their regular life and go on a sabbatical, then come back and re-invent their life.

I had never planned to go back for an advanced degree, but I was interested in aging, the body, and learning in later life, and I wanted to be a better writer. I heard about the master's program at a local college in human development where I could set my own agenda on aging and body wisdom. Almost simultaneously I learned of a master's program in creative writing being offered at another local college. A feeling came up inside me that I could do both of these programs. I could study aging and the body and older adult learning, and I could learn more about creative writing so I could do more meaningful and powerful writing on these topics. It all happened within a week. I registered for both programs.

I was completely rested, eager, and ready to go. I couldn't wait to dive in. It took me a long while to get through both programs—over five years. All of this was very life changing. I really stepped into an ownership of who I am. It all came together for me in my life and in my work, and the result was that I wrote the book, *The Secret Wisdom of a Woman's Body.* Having taken both courses of study gave me new skills for distilling my thoughts on body wisdom, aging, and creativity. It took my writing to a different level, and my new confidence assisted me in presenting what I know in a meaningful, personal way to others.

I think I have a clear and honest assessment of my personal creativity. There are two areas of my life in which I feel I'm creative and productive. One is my writing. Most of my adult life I've been writing: books, articles, and essays. But it wasn't until I pursued a master's degree in writing that I took a closer look at the creative aspects of writing to understand how to express my own voice.

I had been doing most of my writing for other people over the years. Then, nine years ago, I became the editor of a small local paper, and I had the opportunity to write editorials and express my own opinions. I didn't really know how to do that. What do I say? How do I do this? I was really scared to express my own voice. That was the biggest challenge of taking on that job. I could easily edit the paper, no problem doing that, but to put my voice out there, to explore within myself what I have to say—that was an enormous challenge. I was finding myself, finding my voice. And then I took on studying for a master's degree in writing, where I found even more of my own voice. That was exciting and creative. I found something inside of myself that I hadn't ever put on the page.

The other area of creativity that I've developed is in creative movement and dance. This mode of creative expression actually was completely foreign to me. I had no experience in dance. I still can't waltz or do the tango decently, but I can move expressively. As part of my focus on body awareness work I developed an interest in creative movement. Seeing what the body wants to express externally in movement is a true connection with the inner body. Little by little I started teaching workshops around body themes and creative movement. I found so much personal joy in teaching other people as they explored a new way to express themselves. I was teaching in colleges and community settings, community centers, and almost any venue where there was room to move.

As I approached 60, I realized that I wanted the second half of my life to be something new, different, and challenging. I started looking around at how others were creatively re-designing their lives, and I joined a national creative arts and aging network. Out of that grew my current focus of organizing a statewide group in affiliation with the national group. I took on an active role in that group in my state. I travel to various cities and smaller towns, meet and talk with people who never believed arts and creativity had anything to do with their lives. It's stimulating and exciting to witness how the idea of exploring personal creativity in mid-life and the years beyond has caught on.

I really got excited recently when a woman in her 80s came up to me after I'd spoken and said, "How about starting a movement group here in our neighborhood?" If the opportunity seems appropriate after a presentation, I ask if there might be interest in my organizing a memoir-writing group at the community center. It's a joy to watch people getting involved and connected. It's an idea that offers something to a wide range of ages, and the best part of the idea is that talent isn't essential.

We think of our body as a machine that we have to keep tuned up and moving. There's a lot of good information available about keeping the body healthy and active. That's very important, but what I'm talking about is beyond that. Emotional and spiritual truths are sitting right under the skin and trying to get our attention. Many of our health problems come from emotional stresses that get in the way of maintaining our health and our ease of living. It's not just tending to the body in the physical sense but learning to understand the effects of tension, stress and other negative emotions

Many of our health problems come from emotional stresses that get in the way of maintaining our health and our ease of living.

we hold in our bodies that we're not always consciously aware of. Too often we seek out a pill or a formula to fix ourselves quickly, a short recipe for success. But understanding your body isn't a quick fix. It's not that kind of process. It's learning how to quiet the mind, listen to the body, and integrate what your body can tell you.

When I began to listen to my body, I discovered that I was always trying to push things, take on too much and overschedule. I didn't know about going with the flow. I was always in the hurry-up mode. My body listened to my mind, and most often my mind said, " I've got to hurry up, I've got to push," and my body accommodated by pushing. Over time, my body gave back signals, saying, "Hey, this isn't working. Pay attention to me, or I'll break down." My body was constantly in hurry-up mode, and this landed me in the hospital a couple of times. I was lucky. I didn't have an actual heart attack, but an irregular heart beat. The big challenge in my life is to take charge of the feeling of rushing that permeates my whole being, my whole body.

There's a price to pay for not listening to what our bodies are saying. Now, when I notice I'm rushing around like crazy—loosing my keys, forgetting things, pushing in my old pattern—I know my mind is wrong and my body is right, and I need to slow down, let go, alter my pace, listen to what my body is saying. When I'm aware, really awake to what my body is saying, I can smile, be amusing, and, most importantly, pay attention and change my behavior. I haven't completely mastered this; sometimes I don't listen to my body. But that's why I keep teaching others to hear what their body is saying. I need to keep aware and pay attention to my own body, because if my mind totally takes over, the pace gets frantic, overloaded, pressured, and I'm back in my old pattern, and I run the risk of going to the hospital again.

I get a lot of joy from bringing the creative arts network to people, and I love speaking and doing workshops on whole body wisdom. I want to work primarily with women—to help women make friends with their bodies and feel at home in their bodies. As we get older, our bodies are not appreciated and honored in our culture, and we run the danger of taking on this negative attitude towards ourselves. I've learned that I can turn this around, and I want to other women to do this as well.

My groups are mostly women in their 50s, 60s, and 70s. We use our bodies to tell stories. We're constantly in awe at how intimate, creative, spiritual, and emotionally freeing these sessions have become. We talk about how freeing it is for us to move through our day when we're conscious of our bodies. I continue to seek out opportunities to tell others the same thing I tell myself: not to get bogged down in dogma or absolutes, to meet life as it comes, to stay flexible, and to keep moving.

I'm very different than I used to be. I'm more open to see the good in everything. Everything is a gift. I believe it's my vision and my mission to help people discover the gift they are and the gift that life is. I'm learning to appreciate myself and to help others do the same. The true gift is to come into a time of life when you can learn to say, "Here I am," and truly believe you have something to contribute. A lot of us grow up with ideas of who we are and who we aren't, and some of those ideas are not very flattering. I don't think I'm alone in this. I think the hardest part has been for me to accept myself.

There are stories in our bodies that can be expressed in whatever movement form we choose. Not that we don't have pains and illnesses and some real challenges as we age, but when we make friends with our bodies and listen to them, it opens up tremendous possibilities for creativity and healing. This is what I want to support for others, and keep remembering and reinforcing for myself.

Creative Energy flows through me now for my own greatest good and for the greatest good of all.

– Rabbi Ted Falcon

AFTERTHOUGHTS

During my interview with Pat, I was particularly struck by her idea of taking a sabbatical—temporarily leaving much of regular life on hold and throwing out the to-do list. What an amazing idea! If something is less full, there's room for something new to come in. Like most people, I would find it difficult to stop taking phone calls, drop out of social and work circles, and be alone and quiet most of the time. But following this path led Pat towards growth and change. I'm seriously considering a modified sabbatical for myself. Of course, I need to design it around my priority obligations and certain necessities as Pat did. Maybe Pat's experience offers you a similar challenge.

I've also thought about Pat's experience of learning to listen to her body. I agree with her when she observes that our minds tell our bodies what to do, and rarely the other way around. Like Pat, I have a tendency to push myself. Some nights I literally fall into bed, totally exhausted. Maybe if I could learn to hear my body's language, and give it attention equal to what I give my thoughts, a deeper understanding of myself and my body might be the reward.

Betty (age 88)

Be glad today. Tomorrow may bring tears.
Be brave today; The darkest night will pass,
And golden rays will usher in the dawn.

— Sarah Knowles Bolton

Betty is an energetic and outspoken woman with an important and inspiring story to tell.

My life changed considerably when I began to lose my sight. I had macular degeneration in one eye and glaucoma in the other one. Gradually my sight dimmed. I can't read and can't see faces. I haven't seen my own face in the mirror for almost five years. I've forgotten what I look like because I can't see photos either. Thankfully I still have a very small amount of peripheral sight but I'm considered legally blind.

I can't comb my hair and that's a major frustration every day. I can't raise my arms to do that simple thing because of the pain I have in both shoulders. One shoulder has a torn rotator cuff and the pain in the other shoulder is from a break that didn't heal right. I have about a dozen hats and I wear them when I'm not able to have my hair combed by someone else.

Once upon a time my life was very different. I've traveled a lot; I visited twenty-four countries during an era when you could travel cheaply and have a great adventure. I lived in Mexico for a few years, where I took up collage as a sort of a mini-career for a time. After I moved back to the States I had a busy and interesting life taking classes, writing, doing some travel and becoming involved in many activities and projects that were stimulating and interesting.

When I was younger I worked for a number of years in a government program for women aged 17 through 60 who came from rural areas and wanted to improve their lives. I arranged for their basic education, vocational training and personal counseling. For many years I've studied graphology, and I made use of those techniques in determining what occupation my students would be most likely to succeed at and enjoy–car maintenance, electrical services, clerical work, or some other vocation. I have always been interested in the things people reveal about themselves through their handwriting. A friend calls the fruits of my skill 'ink-sights.' I still have more than a hundred books in my library on handwriting analysis although I can't read them anymore.

I've had two marriages. I divorced my first husband after twenty-seven years. My second husband and I separated many years ago. I have three daughters who live in various locations around the country. My daughter who lives near me helps me a lot. She takes me places, writes my checks, and does things for me that you have to have eyes to do. I have a caregiver that comes to help me do some things I just can't do for myself, such as putting the bottom sheet on the bed, doing my wash, cleaning the refrigerator, and cooking for me. For many years I stayed home with my three girls and mothered them; now things have changes and they're mothering me.

The loss of my sight has affected everything I do, everything that's important to me. When my sight began to deteriorate dramatically I found it excruciating, and I cried for a number of months; I couldn't see and I was utterly destroyed. I had started to write a book at the time, I was active as a handwriting analyst and had recently worked on a forgery case. I was doing a lot of things where my eyes were absolutely necessary. Of course I had to give up driving and that loss of independence quickly changed my life.

The thing I found it most difficult to learn was how to walk with a white cane. That was pure agony, both emotional and physical. It was so humiliating for me to know that people looked at me and most probably thought, "Look at that poor blind old lady." I felt humiliated and embarrassed. I had lost a perspective of myself.

I had been a winner most of my life—president of my high school class, the chosen speaker at graduation, awarded a scholarship to college. Everything in my life kept me feeling like a success. Now I was a loser with a white cane. At the time I had no family nearby. I realized my eyesight was going and couldn't be reversed. I decided to move across the country to be close to one of my daughters. I settled into an apartment in an active senior residence where people fifty-five and older live independently.

Shortly after that move I discovered an extraordinary center for the blind and visually handicapped very near to where I lived. I decided to pay them a visit and explore what they had to offer, and it's changed my life. I signed up to work with a mobility instructor who taught me how to use my cane with greater self-assurance. The kindness and skill of her instruction gave me a new feeling of security. What I learned helped me become competent and feel secure. I was gradually able to let go of that painful feeling of humiliation and regain my confidence. I suspect that I presented myself differently to the world when I felt self-confident because people started to greet me on the street. It began with "Hello"s and sometimes grew into conversations and a new relationships. I began going out on the street, to the store, to the local senior center, and little by little I began to build a new life.

Nowadays I manage pretty much of my life without help. I do my own cooking, and

What I learned helped me become competent and feel secure. I was gradually able to let go of that painful feeling of humiliation and regain my confidence.

when I go shopping at the supermarket somebody always comes to help me. The cashiers and the kids that bag the groceries are like my extended family. People in every store in the neighborhood have been helpful and kind, and also many of the people I meet on the street who stop and talk with me.

I just finished taking a course at the local senior center called "Your Mind is Your Mentor." I've joined a Take Off Pounds Sensibly group and I also take a class at the senior center from a totally blind woman who teaches tap dancing. I'm able to walk to the senior center from where I live. I can't cross streets without help but the senior center is on the same side of the street I live on. I leave my cane at the door and go to a dance class. The teacher takes my hand and I dance with the rest of the group. I get hugs and kind words from so many in that group.

I listen to a lot of books on CD; I listen and learn every day. I miss not being able to read a newspaper and I also miss my old habit of doing the daily crossword puzzle. I listen to the radio and to the news on television. I think about what I hear. I get very angry at injustice, hunger in so many parts of the world, in America as well. I wish I could be more politically active. I feel strongly about politics, the need for change in this country in so many areas; we have to improve our educational system. It's appalling that we have hungry children in America. I have an active interest in the world around me. I cry more easily these days because many things touch me very deeply.

I have a wonderful computer where everything can be magnified. My computer has a program that actually reads to me. I push two little buttons and my computer begins talking. The center for the blind and visually handicapped that helped me when I first came here sponsored me for a state-supported program that sends someone to my home to teach me computer skills. That man came once a week for several months and taught me so many useful things. It opened up my life.

It opened up my life. I have more computer skills now than I ever imagined I could acquire without good eyesight.

I have more computer skills now than I ever imagined I could acquire without good eyesight.

The wife of my computer teacher comes once a week to read to me. I've made wonderful personal friends with this couple and they've enriched my life. These are people I never would have met or known if I had been sighted. I just never would have had any reason to have met them or interacted with them. Now they've become two of my closest friends. I know that friendship works two ways and they tell me in different ways that our relationship, our having become real friends, matters a lot to them.

I realize now that when I was sighted I missed many things that I appreciate only now. I've been enriched by blindness. I truly, truly mean that. I feel touched, deeply touched, about things and people that I would never have known had I not lost my sight, and I empathize more deeply with what's going on in other people's lives. I don't think I would have experienced these connections and emotions if I had remained sighted. My life has been enriched in ways I never could have predicted.

Losing my sight was terrible at first, but it also gave me the opportunity to learn firsthand that people with disabilities can do incredible things. It may seem strange but it's really true—I feel blessed in ways I never would have if I hadn't lost my sight.

So many wonderful things continue to happen in my life; I have fun and feel alive. I have a sharp mind because I keep using it. I'm writing, talking with people, I refuse to isolate myself from the world. At 87, I'm incredibly independent and it's a good time of my life.

Happiness often sneaks through a door you didn't know you left open.

— John Barrymore

Afterthoughts

I'm grateful to Betty for sharing her story with a strong voice and deep sincerity. Certainly it's not always *other* people who are challenged by unexpected, unplanned changes in health and mobility. We're all as vulnerable as Betty whether we're in mid-live, years younger, or in our later years.

I, and so many others, have often repeated that trite but true statement, "It isn't so much what happens to you; its how you deal with it." There are times when each of us might be challenged to cope with painful, difficult, and confusing times.

Whether the negative event precipitating the need for adjustment is acute or chronic health changes, loss of job and income, a death in the family, or any dramatic event that requires a major adjustment, we might do well to learn from Betty's story that, simply put, good can grow out of bad, learning and wisdom can grow in unexpected situations.

Judy (age 66)

*Tell me, what do you plan to do with your one
wild and precious life?*

– from *The Summer Day* by Mary Oliver

**I met Judy when I was attending a session entitled, *On Being
an Older Woman* at an annual meeting of the American
Society on Aging. She volunteered to share a bit of her
personal experience of unanticipated growth into a life of
accomplishment and satisfaction. I knew immediately that
hers was a story I wanted to share with others. A few months
later I met with Judy in her small but efficient apartment in
New York. She had just celebrated her sixty-sixth birthday. The
story of her life filled our conversation. Here's chapter one.**

My former husband and I were sweethearts, I was 16 and he
was 17. After high school we both began taking courses
at our local university. I remember well one day at the end of our
first year of classes. It was summer and we had just picked up our
grades. We drove over to a beautiful lake to take a walk. We talked
about our studies and started to discuss our grades. It turned out
that my grades were considerably higher than his. At that moment
I made a conscious decision that I would never get higher grades

than him again. I don't know what made me think this but it was a powerful internal message that I believe influenced my whole life. For all the years of our undergraduate education I made sure that I never got higher grades than his. He never knew that this was a deliberate plan. Maybe I thought I was supposed to do this to be a good companion and eventually a good wife. I just had some idea in my mind that I should not beat him, that he had to be better, that I had to make myself lesser. Inside of me I'm really very competitive; I wanted to be good, I really wanted to be the best.

I was very physically active, physically strong, played tennis, ran, played in all kinds of sports. I decided to go into physical education and be a gym teacher. I remember when we were sitting with friends I'd often say, "He's the brains and I'm the brawn." I had my own sexist attitudes going against myself! I'm so embarrassed about it now, it's shameful. I've learned a lot since then.

I graduated from the university on Saturday, June 11, 1966, and I got married on the next day. Then we had our children and occasionally one of my siblings came to live with us. The house was always full of people. I was a gym teacher, a wife, and a mom of three children. I thought I had a very good marriage; I thought my life as a wife, mom, and homemaker was exactly what I wanted. Yet I often had a very strange feeling that I was really somebody else, that I was not really me. It was like having a distant relationship from my very own self. This is hard for me to find the right words to explain.

It was sort of like there was another person inside of me wanting to get out. It wasn't that I was unhappy with my life, but it was a strange and disturbing thing to experience. I no longer have those feelings.

My husband and I separated and we later were divorced. He

was very fair in making arrangements to provide appropriately for me and the needs of our college-age children. Chapter one of my life was over.

I was going to be on my own for the first time in my life. My daughter and older son were in college and my younger son was also getting ready to go away to the university. I made the decision that I'd go to graduate school. I applied to four different universities and was surprised to be accepted by all of them. I made a decision to get a master's degree In public administration at the Kennedy School at Harvard. That was the first time in my life that I had ever lived alone. It was an exhilarating experience for me and I'm extremely proud of having earned a degree from Harvard.

That was the first time in my life that I had ever lived alone. It was an exhilarating experience for me ...

I had grown up, married, raised my children and except for the Harvard experience had never been anywhere else. I started to do considerable travel on my own. Later in my life, when I was under the auspices of some of the organizations I became involved with, I did extensive traveling around the world. I've probably been to fifty countries and I've been to every continent except Antarctica. I've even climbed Mount Kilimanjaro. It's a very, very hard climb but I was determined to make it to the top. After that experience I was at a women's event where I talked about my climb. In my comments about the Kilimanjaro climb I remember saying things that demeaned my accomplishment: "It wasn't a climb where we used ropes like real mountain climbers, it was just a walk," and "We took a drug so our blood would have additional oxygen or we couldn't have made it to the top." It was like I was discrediting the amazing accomplishment of climbing to 18,500 feet.

I now take credit for doing the Kilimanjaro climb, going to Harvard graduate school, and other things I've accomplished. I often give speeches to women about how so many of us often discredit what we've accomplished. I tell them that I still sometimes catch myself saying, "Oh, it wasn't that big of a deal," or, "It was just good luck that I could get into Harvard"! It was really, really hard to make that climb and there are very few that are accepted into Harvard graduate school. Now I watch what I say about myself and the tone of voice I use. I pay attention not to be self-deprecating, not to put myself down, but to accept and acknowledge what the world would judge as an accomplishment and what I feel I've earned. I think women put themselves down more often than men do. I've worked hard learning to sit on that immediate reaction to demean who I am or what I've accomplished.

After I graduated and realized that I was on my own, with no family responsibilities to kept me in one place, and I decided to move to another city. I chose one in a warmer climate, with a different style and a more comfortable pace of life. I had a job waiting for me there as a development coordinator for a non-profit agency that dealt with local aging issues.

Judy often talks about her youth, when she enjoyed spending many happy hours with older relatives. She remembers sharing wonderful warmth and happy days with each of her four grandparents. Her choice of companions was always older persons, not youthful playmates. She recalls in her 30's and 40's becoming aware of negative attitudes about aging and observed discrimination against the elderly. Judy was motivated to speak out against ageism and mistreatment of older persons. Her passion on the subject moved her towards a new career.

I guess I've always been somebody who fought for the underdog, and what I could see was that older people were discriminated against, especially here in America where there's such a worshipping of youth. I want there to be more fairness in the world; I believe men and women should have equal opportunities. That feminist viewpoint is very, very strong in me. Older *women* in particular need a champion. As we age we become invisible and our voices are not heard. Ageism and negative views of older women abound, yet we're the ones who live longer; we're the ones who are taking care of those who are ill and frail.

Older women in particular need a champion. As we age we become invisible and our voices are not heard.

I heard there was going to be a special aging assembly sponsored by the United Nations in 2002 and I really wanted to be there. I contacted the U.N. group working on the assembly but they already had their quota of representatives signed up. The chair of that committee suggested I check with the Gray Panthers, who, though invited, had never previously sent a representative to such U.N. events. I contacted them and they agreed to send me as their representative to the conference. I quickly discovered that the concerns of the Gray Panthers are exactly what mine are— ageism, sexism, racism—all the negative things I want to erase from the world. Their priorities were wonderful too—healthcare for all, expansion of Social Security. I supported every one of their major concerns. Their mission is to motivate people to action, and that fit me perfectly, as I'm always motivated to do things, not just talk about it. Their motto, Age and Youth in Action, fits my personal mission perfectly. I had followed the career of their founder, Maggie Kuhn, with great admiration so I was proud to represent the Gray Panthers at the conference.

I started out as a quiet listener, but within a year I was the Panthers permanent representative to the U.N. were I now sit on two panels. I started thinking about how much more active and effective I might be in older women's issues if I lived in New York. Within a short time I was living in Manhattan.

One of the panels I joined was called Girls and Women. It focused on issues pertaining to women of reproductive ages. When I got involved we changed the title of that panel to Girls and Women of All Ages. I became active in both the U.N. Committee on Aging and the Committee on Women, and was offered the chair for the International Day of Older Persons.

At the time I became active, other women from all around the world had been working on issues of women's rights for more than 10 years. In 1988 the group called CEDAW, the Convention to Eliminate of All forms of Discrimination against Women, presented a treaty to the United Nations stating in 28 articles the rights of older women. In subsequent years various other initiatives were taken by the U.N. along similar lines, and they were ratified by the member states, which then began integrating into their laws protections and rights of women.

I've also found ways to experience some of the needs of women first hand. Recently I've been teaching English as a second language. Doing this has made me more aware of migration issues and their profound effect on women of all ages. Ninety percent of my students have come from Korea, with five percent from one of the Asian countries and the other five percent from Brazil, Turkey, and other countries. The challenges the Koreans face in learning English aren't the same as if they were French or Spanish where you have the same configuration of letters as in English. Koreans have an entirely different set of symbols. These people work long hours at a job and come to a four-hour class after that. Recently I was one of the organizers of a special session on the subject of migration and its effects on older women. There was standing room only for the session. I've worked hard just to get those two words – OLDER WOMEN – into proposals, work sessions and treaties. I've always said that whatever is good for aging women is good for all women so there's no good reason not include them.

I'm organizing events all the time. Just last night I staged a "Gray and Green" event with a focus on aging and the environment. Eighteen organizations are members of a coalition, everything from Keep America Beautiful to a senior group that's part of naturally-formed retirement community with a membership of ten thousand. People told me they left the event with new insights and understanding of older person's activism and their environmental concerns. I left with the feeling of accomplishment, knowing I had contributed to the recognition and worth of older women.

I've always said that whatever is good for aging women is good for all women…

I guess I'm one of those people who want to change the world. I really believe we can do that in many little ways. That's who I am now and that's where I put my energy at this time of my life. I'm an activist. I'm now the chair of the national board of directors of the Gray Panthers, an active member of the Granny Peace Brigade, and deeply involved with several aging issues with the United Nations. Now that I'm 66 I'm one of those older women that I officially represent.

I feel like I'm bigger than I used to be; I have more interests and activities that I feel really good about. I like to give; that's a value that shapes my life. I haven't large amounts of money to give but I can contribute my time and my skills. I like to organize, I love putting on special events. I get great satisfaction from inviting people to a meeting with a stimulating speaker and provocative conversation afterward, and everyone leaves having learned something, enjoyed themselves and made new contacts. I use my organizing skills in all of the volunteer activities that I take on. I try hard not to be in competition with women because I think women need to be supportive of one another. I like what I perceive to be a woman's way, which is cooperation.

My life is good. I'm healthy, busy with what I love to do, gratified to feel that I'm making a difference. I remember hearing a saying that fits my life perfectly, "Chose a job you love and you will never have to work a day in your life". My personal life still has some challenges. I guess when I practiced that self-effacing routine with my ex-husband I learned it well. My son was talking to some people about me the other day and when he told them my name one woman said, "Of course I know who she is, she's an internationally known expert on aging." When he told me that story I said something self-deprecating like, "That's a mistake; she can't mean me." I heard myself utter those words and realized that of course it was me. I've slowly been able to let go of that kind of response but every once a while it pops up.

As for my personal life, I have a gentleman friend and we live in different cities. We're both busy people and involved with our work but we talk on the phone and e-mail each other often. We plan times when he'll come to my part of the country or I'll go and visit him. The last time we saw one another was almost a year ago but that's not enough for an intimate relationship. We share ideas and opinions when we talk, but to be honest, I miss the touching, the physical contact of a close relationship. I'm very happy with my life here and he's very content with his life there, and I guess that's more important than getting together on a permanent basis.

Right now I count on myself, but it would be nice if I could look ahead and count on just *one* somebody. I can see myself in a relationship, and I'd be happy if that worked out with the man I'm currently seeing. I feel that I want something special in my life at some time in the future. It could be a one-to-one relationship with a man or maybe some kind of communal living. I know of several communities that have a shared living space for meals and sociability, and individual bedroom, bath and office space. Many people I know in their 60's are actively planning with friends to form such a living situation for their retirement years. Another option I've considered, maybe for ten years from now, would be to move close to where one of my children is living and become more a part of their family. Life offers many choices.

When I look ahead, I think that in chapter three of my life I'll want to live in a different way. I can't know how my health or energy or interests will be, but I'm open to change. At this time I'm living my life alone in a proud and positive way. I'm quite independent and on my own and I have a wonderful circle of friends and activities.

The only thing one can count on is change and I've learned to welcome it. I've been looking forward to being old all of my life. I love being 66. I really love it.

Women hold up half the sky

— Chinese proverb

Be the change that you want to see in the world.

— Mahatma Gandhi

AFTERTHOUGHTS

Judy's story offers inspiration in many areas. Yes, we can make a difference if we follow what we believe with action; and yes, we can pick up the broken pieces from a life-changing event, heal and move on; and yes, we can change a behavior of long standing if we realize that it just doesn't work for us.

Specifically I'm referring to how we speak of ourselves. Judy spent many years using words and phrases to others about herself that were demeaning and self-deprecating. She's not alone in such behavior. I've observed many of us in our later years put ourselves down in some way. I recognize it easily because I, too, in my own way of speaking and thinking, have often discounted myself and my accomplishments. Like Judy, I've wondered if I learned that such behavior was appropriate for a woman in relation to a man and then carried the same self-discounting attitude on into other areas of my life.

I leave you with this challenge. Listen to your words and the tone of your voice when you respond to a compliment, and see it you have, perhaps unintentionally, navigated the small distance between healthy modesty and destructive self-disparagement.

Irene (age 64)

This is the story of Irene, a woman who thought she had everything—a wealthy husband, two healthy sons, a lovely home in the city, a large residence in the country, a busy social life. Like a house of cards, everything collapsed at once. Her husband's investments led to a financial disaster, and her marriage disintegrated when her husband left her for a woman he had been having an affair with for several years. The couple separated, their houses were sold, the boys went away to school, and Irene moved alone into a rented apartment. The financial settlement was far less than she had anticipated. To get extra income, Irene's sometimes profession as a writer became a more serious pursuit. Though these radical changes in her life were unanticipated and at first un-welcomed, they gave Irene the opportunity to figure out who she was—now that she no longer was who she used to be.

> *If life gives you lemons, make lemonade!*
> – Anonymous

The most painful change in my life was the separation from my husband seven years ago. We've lived apart since then and were divorced only three years ago. At the time we originally separated my husband had lost a great deal of his money. We used to be very wealthy, now the separation and a difficult economical situation came together and I felt betrayed. When I learned that my husband had had a much younger girlfriend for many years, I was hurt, lost and quite traumatized. I fell into a big black hole. My two sons were very unhappy so I tried to be strong, although I felt weaker than ever before. I was in shock, lost a good deal of weight, and began smoking cigarettes like mad. I moved alone into an apartment, feeling like I would never regain my self-confidence. I had lost trust in others and confidence in myself. Being on my own at the age of 56, I felt I wasn't worth much. I know

I felt I wasn't worth much. I know now that was kind of an old-fashioned female feeling, yet I feared that being single at that age meant being a loser ...

now that was kind of an old-fashioned female feeling, yet I feared that being single at that age meant being a loser—a betrayed older woman who people would look down on.

Still, I was proud that I could support my two sons emotionally through the separation and divorce. I never reproached or condemned their father. My younger son has kept a good relationship with him, but the older one refused, and still refuses, to see his father with his new girlfriend, who he has now married and fathered a child with. He lives with a great deal of pain over the break-up of our family, and although it was my husband who left, I now realize it was my fault too that our marriage was a failure. With the passage of time I've had the courage to look with painful honestly at my relationship with my husband. I had lost respect for him when he became very overweight and I withdrew from any physical relationship. I know I constantly nagged him about yelling at the boys and I criticized him constantly. I could see he had problems and that we had problems, but I didn't make an effort to help the situation in any way. I accept these painful insights now about the role I played in the dissolution of our marriage. Understanding these things taught me a great deal about myself. It wasn't an easy reality to face.

Many months after our separation I slowly began, with some hesitation and insecurity, to accept my independent life and to understand what I needed to take care of myself. Very slowly a new inner process began. I gradually became more confident and more sure of myself. Accepting the challenge of having to manage my own life helped me grow stronger. The fear that I would be looked down on because I had been left for a younger woman slowly began to diminish. What other people thought when I went places alone began to matter less to me. I began to feel like a different me was emerging.

I began to value my women friends more than ever, to trust them and confide in them. I started traveling with a woman friend who listened to my complaints endlessly and helped me get back on my feet. I began recognizing that my value as a person didn't depend on being with a husband; that even on my own, I was liked by friends who didn't care about social status, and all the attributes and concerns of a wealthy, VIP sort of life that had mattered a great deal to me in my former life.

When I'm with my women friends we laugh a lot about our shortcomings that have to do with getting older and feel a wonderful camaraderie. We support each other with honesty, humor and trust. We care much less what impression we make on others. We have become more ourselves.

Yet I feel unhappy that my youthful looks are vanishing. I had always been a pretty woman and men used to find me very attractive and sexy. That was a source of self-confidence and wellbeing for me and naturally I wanted to retain my youthful appearance. I started to fight my wrinkles with botox and had injections of a preparation that fills in facial wrinkles. It gives my face a smoother look. I also had a minor face lift. I still spend a good deal of money on facial creams and hair preparations to keep my youthful appearance. I dye my hair so the grey doesn't show. I do a lot of sports to keep my body thin and fit and I avoid telling people I'm 63 years old. 63 sounds so very old to me! I don't like to tell lies about my age so when the subject comes up I try to change the subject. I guess I don't dress like other women my age. I feel best when I wear tight black jeans, short boots, and a fashionable cashmere pullover with a T-shirt underneath. To be honest, I want people to think that I'm younger than I am.

I do a lot of sports to keep my body thin and fit and I avoid telling people I'm 63 years old. 63 sounds so very old to me!

I have many fears about aging—physical illness, bad memory, helplessness, weakness and dependency. Losing the respect of others is the worst. That arouses fears in me, so I force myself to go to my fitness class regularly and buy anti-aging preparations. I really work hard to outfox old age or at least delay it. I suspect I really haven't gotten over the fact my husband left me for a younger woman. Yet the other side of having been replaced is that I'm not tied down with a young child as they are. I'm relieved that I don't have to lead a young mother's life with all of those constraints and commitments.

I live in the same city as my 93-year-old mother. When I see her I experience how unhappy she feels about not being able to lead an independent life. My mother is quite an attractive woman. She dresses well and makes lively and interesting conversation. I understand why she doesn't want to admit her age to people she doesn't know. I see how condescendingly some older people are treated and discounted. I think that old people aren't given the same respect they were given a hundred years ago.

My mother is only mobile with a walker or a cane for very short distances. She has to ask me or my sister to do almost everything for her. We really want to help but I know she hates to ask us. We take her where she wants to go, we shop for her groceries, pick up her cleaning and her prescriptions along with everything else she wants or needs. I know that my two sons won't be able to take care of me the way my sisters and I take care of my mother. On the other hand I learned from my mother to associate many positive things with old age; tranquillity, sovereignty, a freer sense of humor, self-recognition, being more relaxed, less easily upset about the mistakes and stupid things people do. My mother has lived through crisis and loss, the death of my father and her sister and brother, being displaced in WW II. She has also dealt with a variety of life-threatening illnesses. She's handled many challenges in her life. I respect and admire her resilience.

I get a warm and loving feeling from taking on some of the responsibility, along with my sisters, for my mother. Yes, often I'm impatient because things go so slow, but on the whole she moves me emotionally in a way she never did when I was younger. I see her from a different point of view and I have great admiration for her. I can smile at her little "personality kinks" and we laugh together. We can also talk about our difficulties back in my younger days without any bad feelings. I see my mother not only as a mother but as a whole person, if you know what I mean. And I thank heaven she's still here.

Irene had mentioned that she was a writer. I wanted to know more about her past accomplishments and how she felt about her writing. She became animated and excited when she started to tell me. She smiled when she spoke and it was easy to tell that writing was more than a hobby for her.

These days an important thing in my life is my work, my writing. It really does fulfil me. It keeps my imagination, my creativity and my grey cells active. It gives me a sense of wholeness, and when I get new ideas I feel very much awake and alive. It's as if my writing and I were partners, accomplices conspiring against old age. Staying curious, interested in people around me, observing, taking note, remembering. My observations are creative nourishment for my writing.

For about twenty years I wrote books on education and the problems and issues of dealing with children through their early 20's. I enjoyed writing those books because they had to do with my own sons and my family. Each book dealt with the different stages that my children were growing through. These were typical "how to" books for parents. I learned a great deal doing research and talking to psychologists, teachers and other parents. When my sons were grown my interest for these topics was over. My last book of that type was about when the children move out and the parents are dealing with what is called the "empty nest syndrome."

From that point on I was free to explore other subjects. For much of my early life I lived with my mother, father and sisters in South America, and I have always felt that my roots were in that part of the world. I began travelling to various South American countries and wrote portraits and biographies of Latin American women. My book, *Women of Havana* portrayed the lives of fourteen Cuban women. Another book grew out of travelling to Colombia. I explored the life history of a young Colombian guerrilla-fighter who I interviewed for many weeks in a women's prison. She had been sent there after being caught by the Colombian military. Writing these two books was wonderfully satisfying for me. I was energized from the first to the last minute while working on them. They had to do with my identity, my "inner being." I became lasting friends with all of these women.

I've recently taken on an editing job for someone else's book. It's a series of interviews with business executives about handling stress. I took the job for the money. I edit and edit and there seems to be no end to it. The work is not creative, I can't play or experiment with language as they're not my interviews, and

Writing can feel very lonely sometimes, and I have to be on guard against feelings of being cut off from the life outside.

there's no place for ideas of my own. I'll never do this kind of a job again—unless I'm extremely short of money, which can always happen these days. Editing someone else's book is like putting a lid on creativity. Now I have almost no time for my own writing.

I've never actually made much money on my writing, I couldn't pay my rent if I had to live on my writing so I'm grateful that I have other income to supplement my work. Writing is my passion, my therapy; it makes me feel good inside and very much alive. Sports and writing seem to activate my positive hormones. I overcome sadness best by sitting down and trying to put new ideas into writing. That doesn't mean I don't sometimes draw a blank when I write. Often I sit in front of my computer and nothing comes, but I know that's also part of the process.

Writing can feel very lonely sometimes, and I have to be on

guard against feelings of being cut off from the life outside. In the solitary quiet of the room a hundred doubts pop up and I sometimes wonder why am I doing this? There are so many good writers, why don't I quit and do something useful—and with guaranteed income? Then I go to my exercise class and while I jump up and down and throw my legs in the air my brain fills with wonderful new ideas. Before the day ends I start writing and once more I feel centered and creative.

I've come to understand that writing is something I can do no matter how old I am. I'm just as good at writing as I always was, actually I'm better. Of course I won't quit. I have the chance to write and think and create without having to feel guilty about dishes in the sink, making dinner for a family, or other household tasks waiting to be done. I can do them any time. My life alone offers me that luxury and I can sit down and write for as long as I want.

At this point the phone rang. Irene told the callers she'd get back to them shortly. I asked one last question. "What do you want to tell me that we might have overlooked?"

I suppose before we end our conversation I could tell you about the man in my life. He's younger than I am and it's an uplifting, positive, reassuring feeling to be with him. I get real pleasure having sex with him. I actually enjoy sex more than I did when I was younger. That's really a surprise to me. However, I don't see this relationship as a permanent, long-term commitment. We have very different lives behind us and great differences of opinion, values, and outlooks on life. To commit to living with him or consider marriage I realize I'd have to care enough about the relationship to grapple with a multitude of discrepancies and possible conflicts. I'd have to feel a deeper commitment and love for a person before I'd be ready to take that on.

I no longer need constant social events or other people to fill empty time the way I used to. I've discovered that it's good to become more discriminating as to who I want to spend time with and what places and events I want to attend. I enjoy my own company in a way I never did before. I feel more of an individual, less conformist, and far less dependant on other people's judgements about me. I know now how precious it is that I get along so well with my grown sons and the rest of my family. From the perspective of being older I understand in a new way the value of having my 93-year-old mother and my two sisters around. I value and feel love for my family in a different and deeper way.

When I can't remember someone's name, when I feel my energy becoming less, I do still get a bit anxious. My work helps me feel creative and competent. Writing books has enormous personal rewards. A day of good writing can be more nourishing, more fulfilling, than going out with people with whom I have no close relationship. I can distinguish now between what is important and what is not that important. This has come with growing older.

I've told you a great deal about my efforts to look younger and dress in a way that someone in their 60's might frown upon. I do this because I want the respect and attention that a younger woman gets. Inside of myself I've accepted and even welcomed my new maturity. I don't recall who said that "getting old is not for cowards," so now I am trying to be brave and not a coward. On the whole I do feel more "myself," more accepting of myself, than when I was married and the wife of a wealthy man. Now my self-image isn't borrowed, not validated by having a husband. I feel proud having come this far in seven years without falling apart emotionally. I've grown into myself, and who I am now is more real, and more my own.

> *However confused the scene of our life appears... it can be faced, and we go on to be whole*
>
> – Muriel Rukeyser

AFTERTHOUGHTS

Irene's situation was all too familiar to me, painfully familiar, as it paralleled in some ways a situation in my own life. It takes time to heal from the betrayal of a husband. Yes, mine left me and our children for the woman he married immediately upon our divorce. And indeed it took honesty and courage to get past the hurt to look at my own role in the disintegration of our marriage. My conversation with Irene took place only 7 years after the split from her husband. She already is on her way to a new understanding of herself, growth, maturity and self-understanding.

There is no magic formula for healing in such situations. My healing was slower, many smaller steps along the way to knowing who I could become and how I could get there. I didn't reach out to friends, as it was a time when no one I knew had experienced separation or divorce. I knew I needed perspective and support and finding appropriate professional help sustained me through a long period of healing, growth, self-understanding and acceptance. This was a time of major disruption in the pattern of my life. The challenge was life-changing.

There's no formula for recovery or acceptance, for

integrating an experience and moving on. We each must follow our own timing, our own way of being, of finding who we are now. So many women I've spoken with have told me that out of the chaos of some tragedy or major disappointment have come discoveries of skills, talents, and new interests that lead them toward new careers, hobbies, friends and recreational activities. I'd like the think that Irene's story of determination, resilience, and growth might offer you inspiration and comfort during times of personal challenge. There's hope in what one woman called "my personal collection of catastrophes!"

Kate (age 58)

*Begin somewhere; you cannot build a
reputation on what you intend to do.*

— Liz Smith

I met Kate one evening when I was traveling and checked into
a quaint and quiet Bed & Breakfast. She was managing the
B & B for her mother who owned and ran the charming and
cozy establishment. We started talking, laughing, and sharing
opinions on many subjects; tea and cookies followed. There was
instant rapport between us although she is 58 and I'm 20 years
older. Kate openly began to talk about her past experiences and
her present commitments.

I had one of my recording devices with me and I asked her
if I could turn it on and possibly share her story with others;
she graciously consented.

Sometimes we meet someone unexpectedly and in a brief
conversation we not only learn about them, but if we really
listen, really hear, we learn something about ourselves. Such is
the power of story.

I can summarize my earlier years in a couple of sentences. I discovered very early in my life that I had a talent for drawing. I

studied painting and drawing in college and got a lot of attention and praise for my work. I fell in love quite young, got married and had a daughter. The marriage didn't last. I raised my daughter as a single parent. When my daughter was in high school she decided she wanted to live with her father, his second wife and their family.

Having come into a new independence when my daughter moved allowed me to think in terms of a new kind of freedom. Although my friends and family expected I'd pursue painting, that didn't happen. I had developed an interest in the theater and in cooking. I don't know if I was very lucky or very persuasive but I was able to convince a renowned French chef to allow me to apprentice with him. I put my interest in theatre aside for a couple of years and devoted myself to training in classic French cuisine. As a result I was able to get employment in a well-known French restaurant and later at a private French club. I thrived on this new profession.

My other interest was in the theater, and as I didn't have to be at my job until later in the day, I joined up with a small troop of actors. We performed for grade school children in the mornings. I never had any theater training but performing came naturally to me. Maybe I wasn't very accomplished as an actor but the troop accepted me and the young children in the audience weren't too critical.

One day the manager of the French restaurant announced they would be closing. The theatre couldn't pay me enough even if I worked full-time for them. While I was thinking about what to do next, something unexpected happened. I got a phone call from a friend of mine who was the casting director for a film that was to be made in the city I was living in at that time. She asked me if I could be available to work with her, as they needed to cast several local actors and I had come to know many of them in the area. Shortly after that production ended another movie shoot came to town and I was given another casting job. I came home at night totally exhilarated with filmmaking and my work in casting. I realized that I was really good at this. I guess I was bitten by the bug. This was the work I decided to pursue.

I was able to get several jobs casting films in succession—it amounted to regular employment—and I loved it. I'm a quick "people reader" and that's a skill you must have to do casting successfully. I have an instinct for a person's ability to transform into another character. I had worked hard to develop this skill and I earned visibility and reputation in this field. I worked on location often and traveled a great deal.

After a few years I settled down and opened my own studio in San Francisco. It turned out to be a permanent move. I was the principle casting director on many films and I was able to give a lot of people work. I took occasional trips back east to where my mother lived after my father passed on. My work consumed me and except for seeing my mother and my now married daughter on those brief visits, I was very busy with my own life. I did auditioning and casting for more than twenty years. I loved my work and these were happy years for me.

Before I turned on my recording device Kate began to tell me about her mother and the circumstances that put her in charge of the bed & breakfast.

For many years Kate's mother, who is now in her late 80's, has owned and personally managed the B & B. It's located on the main street in a rural suburb of a large eastern city. Through the years it was frequented by travelers who had not

only heard of the charm of the place, but of the dynamic lady who ran the business.

Kate told me the story of her last visit home, when her mother's friends took her aside and shared their observations and concerns. Her mother's memory loss had progressed and macular degeneration had become a major disability as well. They insisted that the car keys be taken away so her mother could no longer drive. The friends also strongly suggested that someone in the family move home, supervise the care of their mother, and manage the bed & breakfast. Kate told me that it was the first time she became aware of the dramatic decline in her mother's mental and physical condition. There were serious decisions to make.

My siblings were all married, committed to work, as I was, to their lives and families in other cities. My career was going strong and I wasn't anxious to make a change. I knew someone had to do something quickly. After returning home I'd sleep fitfully, toss and turn most of the night. I'd get up in the morning exhausted and stressed. Yet I continued to say to myself, "I just can't make the move back to my home town; I can't make such a drastic change, my life and work are here, I can't assume that responsibility; I don't want to do this." I kept thinking of every reason why it wouldn't work for me to take on what I could clearly see was needed. This

I kept thinking of every reason why it wouldn't work for me to take on what I could clearly see was needed.

negative thinking paralyzed me. I was stuck; it wasn't resolving anything for me, my siblings, or my mother.

One day I said to myself, "I can't go on thinking like this, it's getting me nowhere, I've got to come to some decision and come to a place of peace within myself." The very next morning I woke up with determination to seize the day and change my conversation with myself. I started both thinking and saying, "I'm healthy, look at what I have, I can handle this responsibility. I've invented this life and I can create a new one, I can create a new reality." My thinking changed from negative to positive when I changed my thinking and decided I'd move back to the other end of the country. It made all the difference. I began making plans to close my business, pack up and move back into the family home. These past couple of years I've taken on the responsibility of my mother's care and managing her business.

I have a strong sense of duty. Maybe I have a stronger sense of family duty than my siblings do, or maybe it was just an easier decision for me to make because there was nothing tying me down except I had established myself in the film world. Yet in the back of my mind I believed that I had a profession that I could find a way to transplant. I felt that somehow I could find a way to continue my profession and sustain my career three thousand miles away from the center of the movie world on the West Coast.

I wasn't surprised that Kate was making coffee and baking muffins in the kitchen of the bed & breakfast at 6 o'clock the next morning. After the office and cleaning help arrived, Kate left for her "full time work" at her acting and casting studio.

My reputation has followed me and I found it possible and actually profitable to operate an acting studio here. I train young actors and I have contacts established to do casting. One of my students had a large role in a major film last year and another of my students had a role in this year's Academy Award winner. Those young people had been training with me for more than two years. I've brought my life across country with me and replanted it.

This work is so rewarding and rich that everyday I see results. I audition potential students and only take them if I sense the determination in attitude and their ability to take their training seriously. I'm not interested in working on an amateur level; I've been in the professional world too long. My school is important for me; it has allowed me to bring my career with me while also taking care of my mother and running the bed and breakfast.

After I moved back home my mother expressed a desire to involve all of her children in her future care. A lawyer drew up papers assigning each of her five children some portion of the responsibility for her care, money, investments, and property. Each of them signed an agreement that expressed her wishes and yet, over these past two years not one of them lived up to the responsibilities assigned in that agreement. I recently called together the whole family and read the document aloud. I've had to be a sort of a fighter, a leader in the family and now, finally, each of them has taken on their assigned responsibility and it makes it quite a bit easier for me. I didn't enjoy this coordinating role but I do feel good that I could pull the team together.

One day Mother said, "Kate, I knew you would be the person that could organize the family. You know who you are and exactly what you want." That moment was a bonus because my mother's lucid moments are few and far between. It was such a reward to have her realize that I understand myself and accept what my strengths are at this stage of my life. I'm not only getting to know my mother during this time but I'm discovering another part of myself.

Recently I arranged for a friend to move into my mother's home so she now has someone there over the dinner hour and through the night. For now this new arrangement works. I see my mother once or twice during every day. I often take her out and we just do simple things like trying on hats in one of her favorite stores. I feel it's important for her to laugh, to enjoy herself. Flexibility is a necessity. It's not possible to know how mother's mental and physical health with be in the future so I literally live one day at a time.

Since I've taken on this role I've learned things about myself I never experienced before. I've discovered another layer of myself. I've also learned another side of my mother. I've always loved my mother but I never thought of her as a friend that I would share confidences with like a best friend. Our relationship is very different now. There's a new comfort between us. I actually have patience with her, which is something very new for me. I'm learning every day how to understand her world as she sees it, a world that has changed very much for her.

I've found that the greatest gift I've been able to give my mother is just to listen. It's given me a way to understand her and her shifting moods, and it's also given me insight into her feelings and concerns. I used to be talking all the time and not listening. It's not an easy thing for people to really deeply listen. I understand now how important listening can be. I have 50 students in my acting school who range in age from 8 through 18 and I've also learned to listen to them. I've become a very good listener. The person talking knows if you're really listening and it can be a

These days I'm able to empathize with other people rather than thinking only of my own reaction to things. This is a big change for me.

real gift to give someone, a gift of openness and caring about what they're sharing. In that way I've grown and matured a great deal.

These days I'm able to empathize with other people rather than thinking only of my own reaction to things. This is a big change for me. I certainly have to do that with my mother. That's how I can accept whatever mood she's in, understand what her priorities are and let mine go when I'm with her. I've learned a lot being with my mother this past couple of years. I relish the time with her. There's some bitter-sweet of course as I see my mother fading.

There's something about how I'm living today that has given me a new inner calm I've never experienced before. I don't try to force things to happen; I have a new comfort in "going with the flow." I don't push things as I used to do. I don't force things to happen, and if they don't happen, nothing lost. I'm just in a very calm and grateful place in my life and there's great comfort in just accepting that. Yes, this is a completely new pattern for me.

I've also learned to change my pace. I'm not in the fast lane any more. I have to go with my mother's rhythm, whatever it is on this day, and be flexible enough to change pace completely tomorrow if her mood and energy are drastically different. I want to take each day as it comes. I want to be available and open to becoming more self-aware. I'm in a growth period at this time in my life. I feel open to these changes and welcome them. It's like some dust has settled and I'm able to be in the flow. I have a new clarity.

It's important for me to tell you that I'm really grateful for the opportunity to be here for my mother. It's a time in her life when she often feels confused and fearful and it's good for us both to feel close to one another. Almost every day I hold her hand and tell her, "Don't worry, Mom, whatever needs to be taken care of I'll do it and I'll take care of you and everything will be alright." She hears the truth in my voice and it's a comfort to her. This is my first experience in caregiving. When my father was ill with cardiac problems my mother took care of him; all of us children were living somewhere else.

I know how important it is at my age to take care of myself and sustain my energy and stay in good health. I go to bed by 10. I know I have to watch what I commit to because I have to get up at 5:30 every day to get the morning meal started. My day is long and full. I develop my mind too, of course. I learn new things every day. I challenge myself intellectually and I read a lot and I keep my mind learning and expanding. But most importantly for me, I'm always working on what I call my feeling center. My personality, my motivations, my ideas, and my whole creative self radiates from a place inside me that I call my feeling center, my emotional center.

For now, I've totally embraced my new reality, which is about work and family. But I'm aware that this isn't going to be my life forever. As sentimental as my mother is about the B & B, she's consented to sell it if an appropriate customer comes along. She does insist that the new owners commit to keeping the charm she's created here. It's been her life. When my mother isn't here anymore and the bed & breakfast is sold and I no longer have that responsibility, then I'll re-design my life again. My life has had many chapters and there will be more. I'm ready to embrace whatever comes along in my life. I'm a "yes" person, That's my favorite word; yes I can, yes I will, yes I want, yes I'll go through that next door. I'm not afraid of change.

My new mantra has become, "What a great place to be, I have so much here, it's really a beautiful place." I love the change of seasons, I so much enjoy watching the students in my acting school develop and fulfill their dreams. And I also get satisfaction from the fact that I'm a support and comfort for my mother. Our relationship is so different now. It's truly my pleasure to be here and help my mother. This is a good time of my life.

> *True wisdom lies in gathering the precious*
> *things out of each day as it goes by.*
>
> — E. S. Bouton

Afterthoughts

So many of us have been, or may be at some future time, torn with confusion and anxiety when we're called upon to play a role of primary caregiver for a loved one. Your situation may require changing a work schedule, juggling meals or transportation schedules for your family, or recruiting other relatives and friends to help, as we incorporate our new responsibilities into our ongoing life.

Such changes are demanding, exhausting and difficult. They may involve moving to another part of the country, giving up a job or an established career, or leaving good friends; all major life changes.

Each of us who faces the challenge of being middle-aged children with aging parents with have unique and particular family concerns and circumstances. I wanted to share Kate's story as one example of embracing the care-giving role, not just as a worrisome, emotional and painful disruption in one's life, but as an opportunity for learning about oneself and others, growing in wisdom, understand, and depth.

June (age 66)

*I believe the most important thing
beyond discipline and creativity is
daring to dare*

— Maya Angelou

Sometimes you hear a story about an ideal family—a mother who provided every opportunity for her daughter, gave her every educational advantage, provided love and encouraged her to follow her dreams. How lucky this young person would be if she wanted to grow up to be a doctor, a respected surgeon and teacher at a major university medical school. We'd be happy for her of course.

When I met Dr. June I was impressed with her position and accomplishments. The story she shared with me has the same ending as the one I've just described but not the same beginning. The story of how Dr. June realized her dream can offer inspiration to every woman who has goals, hopes and dreams—but a less-than-ideal family environment within which to pursue them.

My personal goals and desires are more modest than Dr. June's. Yet I draw inspiration from her determination, clarity of purpose and willingness to learn from experience. Whatever your particular challenges might be, I hope that you, too, might be inspired by the example of someone with the confidence to realize dreams that at times seemed far beyond her reach. Here's June's story.

I grew up on a farm; my father farmed but he hated it. He had been a tree trimmer until he fell from a tree and couldn't do that kind of work anymore. My grandfather owned several farms so my parents decided to move to one of them. They didn't have any money, but it was a good life for me. I didn't know we were poor because I always had enough to eat and my mother sewed my clothes.

My father was clinically depressed. I remember he was hospitalized and had electric shock treatments but it didn't help much. I know my mother had been mentally abused; I don't really know if she was physically abused. When I was about five my mother left my father and took me with her to California to live with my grandparents. In the life of farm people there wasn't such a thing as divorce in those days so we eventually moved back to the farm. In the 1940's and 50's you stuck it out in a marriage.

I was totally oblivious to what was going on in my parents lives. My father committed suicide when I was 16.

It was around that time that I met the young man that was to become my husband. He loved to hunt and fish, very much like my dad actually. He was 24 and I was 17. I was engaged before I finished high school.

After my father's death, my grandpa told my mother that he'd sell her the farm for one dollar so she wouldn't have to worry about finances. Once she owned the farm she decided to sell it, go to school and get a cosmetology license and open a beauty shop in the small town where we lived. My mom also encouraged me to get training for an occupation of some kind so that if my husband died I'd have something to fall back on.

Her bold actions following my father's death were an example for me, giving me encouragement to follow my own personal dreams and ambitions.

Following her mother's sensible example, June registered for classes in a nearby city. Her interest in chemistry led her into training to be a lab tech and x-ray technician.

I came back home from my classes every weekend so I could see my fiancé. When I graduated I was qualified to be employed as a lab and x-ray technician, and I easily got a job doing the lab work I was trained for. I really enjoyed it. My boyfriend and I were married and I wanted to have a family but I couldn't seem to get pregnant. We decided to adopt and our family started with a beautiful baby boy. After we had been married for ten years I became pregnant, to my great surprise, and I was even more surprised when I became pregnant again almost immediately. Those two boys are only 15 months apart. I continued to work at my lab and x-ray tech job, my husband owned and ran a small service station, we had three beautiful boys, and I was content with my life.

After a time, though I loved the lab and x-ray work I was doing, I became unhappy with my particular job situation, and applied for a class to become a physician's assistant. My application was rejected because I didn't have the prerequisite education—two years of college. No one in my family had ever gone to college but I was determined to get in that physician's assistant training.

By that time I had worked as a lab technician for ten years. I went to each instructor and explained that I was paying for my own education, that I would be commuting 2-3 hours a day to class, that I had 3 kids at home, and that I was certain that I would succeed. I asked each instructor to just give me a chance—and they did. At the end of the first quarter I had a 4.0 average and I graduated in two years.

The only way I've gotten anywhere is by taking risks. I was gratified that I took this one.

With my new training I got a job as a physician's assistant for two doctors that paid a good deal more than my previous position. I worked in their clinic for almost 18 years. I enjoyed my work and thought I was doing a good job, although I didn't get along well with one of the physicians. One day they told me that they could no longer afford me and that they were terminating my job, not soon but immediately. It was totally unexpected. I was shocked. I didn't really accept their reason, yet I was so confused at that moment that I didn't think to question them further.

The only way I've gotten anywhere is by taking risks. I was gratified that I took this one.

For some period of time I had serious disagreements and unpleasant conversations with one of the doctors, and our working relationship had deteriorated. It seemed clear to me that the explanation of finances was only an excuse.

The abrupt termination left me extremely angry and humiliated in addition to the stress of losing my income. That very same week my husband went into a chemical dependency counseling program that he had previously resisted for some time. He and I had been growing apart for several years and it was during that same week that we began to discuss the possibility of divorce for the first time. It seemed my whole world was falling apart. I had never before in my life felt as confused and overwhelmed as I did at that moment. I had never chosen to seek professional help before, but I was devastated and immediately sought out help. My therapist was an important part of my growth and healing. I desperately needed someone to talk with, someone who would be patient and listen to me. Entering into that dialogue helped me listen to myself. I came to realize that I had reached a point in my life where I was ready to take another risk.

This was a pivotal time in June's life. Crisis opens possibilities of going in many directions. June made the decision not to run away in spite of her impulse to do so. Instead, she began to move forward toward newly-formulated career ambitions.

My interest in working in the field of medicine was strong. After much serious thought I knew I wanted to go to medical school. I realized that I didn't have the college education necessary to apply to medical school but I wasn't going to let that discourage me. My sister-in-law offered to help with my kids so I began exploring how and where I could get the education I needed. Within two months I registered in summer school at a large university—a daily commute of two hours. I joined a carpool with three other students and if it wasn't my turn to drive I sat in the back seat and studied the whole time.

On the first day of one class the instructor said, "You all have to be here to take all exams, there will be no excuse. Anyone who doesn't show up gets a failing grade." One exam morning I woke up to discover there had been a severe ice storm. I didn't have any driving companions that day so I had to drive alone. It was a long, dangerous trip; it took almost three hours for me to reach the campus. When I got to the classroom I discovered that because of the severity of storm they had cancelled all classes.

While attending that university I also broke my ankle and went to classes for six weeks on crutches. It wasn't easy for me but I was determined to complete my studies.

To avoid the long commute, I eventually rented an apartment near the university with a woman I had met who, like me, was completing her education in her middle years. I was returning home on weekends and it was working out sort of OK, but at the end of one semester I could see I was running out of money. I didn't know what I was going to do. My roommate was in the midst of a divorce from her husband who was a doctor. They were still on good terms and she wrote to him asking if there was any way he could help me secure financial aid to stay in medical school. One day he called to suggest that he and his partner loan me whatever funds I would need to continue my studies. The loan was to be interest free as long as I was in school and 6% after graduation. I have a tremendous feeling of gratitude for the support that I got from those two doctors. I don't know how I ever would have continued my studies without their help. It gave me the financial support I needed and reinforced the feeling that my pursuit of a career in medicine career was the right path.

It took me two years to complete the required studies. I took chemistry, physics, calculus, organic chemistry, and English composition. It was a whole new experience for me. One event sticks in my mind. At the end of the first week of English, we were all required to write a two-page paper. The next day the instructor asked me to stay after class. I was very anxious. I knew to get into medical school you had to do well in all subjects. I waited rather apprehensively after class. The instructor took me down to her office and showed me the rest of the papers that had been turned in. It was unbelievable. There were papers written in pencil, pages torn out of notebooks with the shredded sides hanging. Some of the students couldn't construct a sentence, others used colons and semi-colons in totally inappropriate places. The whole batch was awful. The instructor said, "You're wasting your time in this class." I told her that I couldn't get into medical school without an A in it. "I understand," she said, "Here's your assignment. Write a final paper. This is a remedial class. You don't need to be in this class again."

My other prerequisite courses gave me little trouble. I got my straight A's. The real competition came when I made it into medical school.

When it came time for me to apply to medical schools, only two were close enough to be feasible, which limited my chances of being accepted. I clearly remember getting the letter from the local major university medical school telling me that I was accepted. Other than the birth and the adoption of my children it was the most exciting day of my life. My mother and my best friend were very happy for me; my husband wasn't happy at all. So I was conflicted. I didn't want to uproot my children from their school and their friends and my husband absolutely refused to move closer to the university. The only alternative was to live on campus and return home on weekends. My husband and I hadn't separated yet but it wasn't much of a marriage at this point.

During the whole time I was in medical school I was blessed with a sister-in-law who lived just across the park from us. She offered to take care of my three boys, get them off to school, and be there for them when they came home. She was absolutely wonderful. I know I couldn't have done it without her help. I guess any mom taking so much time away for themselves would be conflicted and I certainly was. I remember the first time I left the boys with her. I drove home anxiously, worried that the arrangement wouldn't work out, but when I arrived they all cried because they didn't want to leave her house and stop what they were doing. After that I quit worrying and began to concentrate on my studies.

During my years as an undergraduate, I was home every night and gave the kids my attention. I didn't study until the kids went to bed. Now my studies required a more intense dedication. I would get up at 3 a.m. on Monday and drive back home after class on Friday. My husband helped out with the kids during the week in spite of the fact that he was terribly opposed to my going to medical school. Maybe he resented the extra responsibility, or felt that my becoming a doctor would bring our worlds even farther apart. I don't know what he was thinking but I didn't ask. I was determined to succeed and it was darn hard for me. I was in my late 30's and I was much older than the rest of the pre-med students, and with all that I was juggling in my life, I was worried I couldn't handle it.

...the university medical school had never taken anybody my age. I was older and in a different situation than anyone else in my class and there wasn't much support.

At that time, the university medical school had never taken anybody my age. I was older and in a different situation than anyone else in my class and there wasn't much support. I didn't have support at home either but I was determined to push on and succeed. I had the encouragement I needed from my mother, my sisters, and the person who had been my therapist during the stress of losing my job as a physician's assistant. She ended up being my best friend and I needed one during this tough and intense period in my life.

During the week, when I was away for four days, I borrowed money and hired a woman to come in and be with the boys when they came home from school, make dinner and get them to do their homework. There were times when I felt so guilty, so guilty. When I was in my first year of medical school I remember one time when I couldn't make it home on a weekend because of the pressure to study for final exams. It was Saturday and I was in the study hall and tears were running down my face. My son was graduating from a Sunday school program and I couldn't be there. When I called home my husband said, "See, I told you it would be like this. Now live with your choices."

The first two years of medical school entailed a lot of memorization. But because I had worked in a doctor's office for so many years, I didn't have to learn how to talk to patients, listen to them patiently, do a history or a physical. I failed one course, bio-chemistry. I had never faced failure any time in my life. I didn't go home that summer. I studied 8 to 10 hours a day getting ready to take a make-up test. The two professors who taught the course were supportive and very generous with their time; if I needed an hour they gave it to me, and I needed lots of hours. When I took the test I passed, and I had learned something about failure. You have to pick yourself up and you have to succeed the second time. Now I sometimes tell my students this story. It's useful to them to know that I struggled with something and by determination turned failure into success.

There's no question that I sacrificed, and my children sacrificed, for me to do what I did. My three boys keep assuring me that it was OK that I was in school, but there were struggles. One stressful and sad experience for our family was when my one of my sons broke into a neighbor's house and took a shotgun. He was in prison for two years. I am thankful that he has since turned out to be a very nice and honorable young man, a good father, and he wants to go to law school. He's checked it out, taken the prerequisites and he's in his middle 30's. I remind him I did it in my 40's. I encourage him to do what is important for him.

Residency was long hours and being on call every other night—in short, it was Hell. As my education and training drew to a close, I started to think about what I was going to do. Originally I was sure my choice would be family medicine but I began to realize that I wanted to specialize in obstetrics and gynecology. The next challenge was to get into a surgical residency at the age of 45. They had never taken anyone that age but yes, I was accepted at the University Hospital that was close enough to permit me to go home one day a week to visit my family.

My plan was to go back to my home town and open an office. I guess we never know what might come into our life to change our plans. When I was 49, and in the last 6 months of my residency, I unexpectedly had an opportunity go to Philadelphia and spend a month at one of the first menopause clinics in the country. While I was there I was exposed to a whole new world of medicine, and when I returned I told the head of the department at our university that they could be doing a much better job of teaching OB-GYN residents about menopause. There are 40 million women out there in need of doctors that understand menopause and women's health. The subject became a passion for me.

When I graduated from medical school my family attended the ceremony. When I was called up to be hooded my son stood up and yelled, "Way to go, Mom!" The whole auditorium cheered.

Shortly after graduation I was offered a job at the university medical school. I had no intention of going into academics but it was an exciting opportunity and I was in the right place at the right time. I thought about the offer and felt that I could have a bigger effect on the lives of women if I took that position than if I entered private practice. A heart and estrogen replacement study was about to start and they needed a gynecologist who could do endometrial biopsies. I said, "Yes".

Shortly after that the Women's Health Initiative was launched and again I said, "Yes". I like to work one-on-one with women but I also discovered that I also liked to teach. My position gave me an opportunity to travel around the country lecturing on menopause, sexual function, and hormone therapy. I felt that I was really doing a good job at it, and I loved my work.

June was productive, stimulated and felt a good deal of accomplishment. Although her education and career came later in life than usual, her so-called mid-life arrived on time. "It was a time in my life when I felt a need to do some serious introspection," June told me. I quickly responded, "Do you mean you were asking yourself, Who Am I Now That I'm Not Who I Was?" We both laughed and then continued our conversation.

By this time my marriage had disintegrated completely and my husband and I were divorced. I loved my work, yet something was missing from my life. I felt the need to do some serious introspection. Friends suggested a seminar course that had such a focus, and although I had never before considered doing such a thing, I registered to take it. The sessions challenged me to look at my life in a way I had never done before. I realized that I still carried a lot of emotional baggage with my ex-husband, and also with the doctors who had fired me many years ago, along with other unresolved issues.

The sessions challenged me to look at my life in a way I had never done before.

I discovered that I was holding a terrible resentment against the doctor with whom I had not gotten along well during my years as a medical assistant. That resentment and anger wasn't hurting him at all; those feeling were only hurting me. In accordance with the requirements of the self-exploration sessions, I contacted the doctor that I had worked for and told him about my long held anger. I told him that for years I hated him. He was shocked. Ironically, if I hadn't left that job and followed my dream of becoming a doctor, my life probably would not have turned out the way it did. I was amazed at the results of the phone call. I was able to easily let go of the strong, negative feelings that I had held on to for so long.

I also went to my ex-husband and told him that although I had once blamed him for everything, I now realized that I also deserved a measure of the blame for our past problems. The most important thing was that we shared three children and grandchildren and I wanted us to be friends. The process was amazing. It seemed like a miracle, no less. As I gave up resenting and blaming, I was able to let all that go. And the desire to revert to such behaviors never has surfaced again.

Another part of the course involved trying to understand what drives me. I've always had this strong feeling to succeed, to be good at what I do. There was a time in my life when I had a driving need to always be right. When people asked me a question I didn't know the answer to it was terribly anxiety-provoking for me. Recognizing that it's OK not to know everything was a very big thing for me. What a relief.

During the three days of the introspection seminar June discovered something else about herself. She started to feel a strong need to share her experiences with someone. Those feelings, which she had previously been unaware of, brought a new element into her life. She met a woman in the seminar and they became friends. As the friendship grew in the months that followed the seminar, the two women moved in together and they lived together for ten years. A sexual relationship with a woman was a whole new path for June.

Prior to that, such a relationship with a woman had never had an attraction for me and hasn't been since. Yet, at the time it was comfortable and easy for me. I didn't feel a need to hide the relationship or deny it. I remember telling my middle son that I really needed to sit down and talk to him. I remember going into a long and detailed explanation about my fear of losing his love and respect and when I finished he blurted out, "Gosh Mom, I thought you were going to tell me you were dying of cancer or some other disease. I've known what you just told me for months!" I guess my family just wanted me to be happy. All of my kids, and my mother too, accepted my new partner into the family.

During the relationship my physical attraction for my partner dwindled, and when those sexual feeling for her disappeared she decided to withdraw from our partnership. I learned something very valuable about myself from that relationship. I wanted to have someone to share my life with. I wanted closeness, friendship, and caring in my life. The woman I was with was considerably younger than I was—twenty years, actually. I now realized that what I really wanted was someone of my own generation, someone who remembers where they were, as I do, when Martin Luther King was shot or who Imelda Marcos was; not specifically those things, but that we have both lived within the same frame of time.

Two and a half years ago I joined an on-line dating program to meet someone. Eventually I began a correspondence with a man who had been widowed for two years. We spoke on the phone every day for maybe a couple of months before we actually met. He matched my age, education, religion, politics, philosophy; everything was compatible except he lived in an adjacent state. Around the third or fourth time we were together I told him about my past relationship with a woman. It seemed to make no difference to him at all. He's very active in the Committee on Ministries and he's very supportive of having gays and lesbians in the ministry.

I wanted to have someone to share my life with. I wanted closeness, friendship, and caring in my life.

I have known the man now for a year and a half, and the two of us are going to be married in a couple of months. A new chapter of my life is ahead, my life as a mature, older woman in her mid-sixties. I'm stiff in the morning these days, my face is getting wrinkled, and I take a collection of pills everyday. I've had five stints placed in my coronary arteries, I've had weight problems all of my life. When I tell my women patients about keeping their weight down I tell them honestly what a struggle that has always been for me.

One thing I've found about aging is that it's very freeing. That started for me at about the age of 50. I dress how I want and feel no need to conform to what other people might think is proper or correct. I wear Birkenstocks all the time. For dress up I have a pair of gold Birkenstocks and a pair in patent leather. I attended one event dressed up in lovely silk suit and my Birkenstocks of course. A colleague of mine came up to me, complimented me on my suit and felt obliged to suggest that I'd look better if I wore heels with my outfit. I replied to her, "Says who?" At the end of the day my feet don't hurt at all. You can't tell me that someone wearing three-inch heels with those fashionable pointed toes doesn't get sore feet at the end of the day. I think this independent attitude that I've developed has something to do with aging. As I've aged I've given myself permission to be who I am. I told the man I'm going to marry about the incident and that I had no intention of changing into someone I'm not. He smiled sweetly and said, "Don't change. I love you the way you are."

I'm taking early retirement. I'll be leaving my position next year. I'm getting really tired of the demands on my time beyond practicing medicine. There are pressures to generate income for the university, and an increasing focus on business which doesn't interest me. I'm certainly not going to stop women's medicine. But I am going to stop having to be at work at 7 in the morning and staying at work until after 7 at night. I'm going to be contributing in other ways.

I plan to write on a website for women's health. I'm looking forward to a new challenge. I'm also going to be doing some research and serious medical writing in the future. I'm passionate about women's health and I'm a great spokesperson for that subject. I can be a strong voice for that cause. Also, my university is about to launch a $900 million campaign for a women's health project and I will be available to help with that.

People often say to me, "I don't know how you did that." I guess I just wanted it badly enough to push through. Others say, "Don't you wish you could have gone to medical school when you were in your 20's?" I say No. I would not have been the same doctor.

It's my experience that has taught me about life. I couldn't possibly have had the insights and maturity when I was twenty that I feel I have now. I hadn't lived enough. I don't consider myself wise, not yet. There are other words that describe me. I'm intense, hard-working, smart, loving, energetic, compassionate, thoughtful and generous. I describe myself also as a skilled surgeon and others refer to me that way as well.

I guess as we get older I'd advise taking chances that are reasonable. When you're younger you can take bigger ones.

I think that each one of us should live our lives to the fullest—in whatever way seems fitting. There's no reason to follow anyone else's way but I encourage others to take a chance in their efforts to achieve their goals. I guess as we get older I'd advise taking chances that are reasonable. When you're younger you can take bigger ones. I guess I was on the border line when I went off to medical school at age 41 but it changed and fulfilled my life, and I have few regrets as I look back.

One big thing I've learned is that the most important people in my life are my family. When I take retirement from the University Medical School, they'll find someone else to fill the position. But I'm the mother to my children, grandmother to my grandchildren and no one else can fill those positions. As I've matured, I realize this is my family, they're mine. In the end, that's who and what really counts. They know that I'm always there for them and they're always there for me.

I'll be getting married soon. I'm praying this relationship works out. He doesn't want to live in the city and I too really love living in the country. So it's another fork in the road. My income isn't going to change very much when I retire. I've invested every penny I've earned in five different retirement plans. I'm hoping that totally changing my life isn't too big a shock. A lot of people have fear of the unknown but I'm feeling something different. It's more like wonder and anticipation. I'm on the cusp of a big change. Yet every time I've made a change in my life, everything has gotten better. I feel really good about my life and about my contributions to the field of medicine. I feel I was very fortunate, but I also know that I worked very hard for everything I have. I really have a good life. I'm so blessed, so blessed.

> *"The future is ours to channel in the direction we want to go...we must continually ask ourselves, what will happen if...? Or better still, how can I make it happen?"*
>
> – Lisa Taylor

AFTERTHOUGHTS

It was a profound experience for me to talk with June about her seemingly impossible story of accomplishment. I've heard many stories of changing careers in the mid-life years but none with such challenging odds for success. The greatest value for me personally is in learning of her determination and persistence. Her story give me inspiration in attempting to attain my own more modest goals.

People have often said that I inspire them because of my

accomplishments. Yet I view some of my past aspirations and accomplishments as less of a stretch than June's. When I took on a major role in broadcasting it was indeed a stretch but I already had college degrees and some experience in radio production and on-air experience. When I became passionate about changing attitudes towards aging and left the best job I had ever held to pursue that interest, I was energetic, determined and only 50 years old. For me those were a couple of life changes that I summoned the courage to take on, yet June had come from a background very different from the profession she aspired to. Yet her will and determination were extraordinary.

Whatever stage of life you're at when reading this story, there most probably are goals you aspire to; going back to school or taking a particular course of study, learning French cooking, taking a drawing or painting course, starting on body strengthening program, or anything else that has appeal.

One more thought. I resonated to June's realization that she wanted a companion to care for her, and to care about; someone to share her life. Also the notion that she didn't seek a relationship to define herself but to deepen her future mutual experiences. So often in our younger years we choose a companion to more completely define ourselves. In her mid 60's June looks at her forthcoming marriage with a new level maturity.

Allison (age 77)

I guess we never know when someone comes into our lives how brief the encounter will be, or how lasting and deep the relationship might become. I met Allison several years ago at a casual lunch with a group of women, never expecting she would become a lasting friend, that we'd experience each others life transitions, face the challenges that life brings, share our stories and concerns with each other as we change and grow. One day she shared a quote that she said perfectly described the person she was now at the age of 77.

Old age I've decided is a gift. I am now, probably for the first time in my life, the person I have always wanted to be.
— **Anonymous**

My life has changed a lot, and yes, I set out to change it when I decided to go back to the university and commit to the level of study required to get my PhD. I certainly wasn't unhappy. I had a rich and productive adult life, a good marriage, and both my personal and work life had really been satisfying and good. Truthfully however, I don't think I ever put myself first until my 60's when I made the decision to study for my doctorate. It was a time in my life when "I" became first for me.

I recall reading a book about time; about how time gets shorter, seems to move faster when we're in our later years. It's my personal opinion that if a person tries too hard to hold on to the identity they've already developed in their life journey, they might miss out on some of the gifts that can be discovered at the later stages of life. Of course you take your past experience with you as you begin to shape yourself into someone new. My experiences, my past learning—all of that has contributed to who I've become and who I'm becoming.

Looking back on my earlier life, I married and had my two daughters after I finished college. I had a long career of counseling and school administration—a job that I held for about 25 years. The major focus of my work was looking at how I could bring everybody to the table – black student's organizations, groups who worked with the physically challenged, women's groups, those with class issues, economic issues. Later I took on a position as a diversity consultant for law firms.

The work that I'm most proud of with the law firms involved creating what was called the minority roundtable. In that situation young Black lawyers at a firm could meet with white senior partners to talk about their sense of self in their work and their attitudes towards working with others at their firm. I believe we generated some meaningful conversations through that roundtable, discussing issues face to face. Such conversations can change relationships and attitudes, even when the issues are unpleasant. It gives people a different perspective when they actually look at one another while they tackle difficult problems and prejudices. Regrettably, when I left that job, nobody took it on.

After my children were grown and married, I started to feel something that others have written about—a sense of liberation, of late life freedom. That feeling grew even stronger in my mid-sixties. When I became eligible for Social Security I left the workplace. I actually felt the need to let go of some of my former identity and move on.

Originally I thought that my doctoral studies would focus primarily on the subject of race. Some of the first papers I wrote were about inequality and diversity, and that was a life-long personal interest as well as an important part of my work. I didn't abandon that focus entirely, but as I became interested in older women, as I was one, my doctoral program broaden to explore the experience of aging among older women of all races.

During those years of my studies, I spent most of my time alone in this small room where we're having this conversation. I call it my study, my private office, my personal place. It's on a different floor in the building where we live. When this space became available I rented it immediately. I had been trying to study and write papers on a desk in the middle of our apartment and it just wasn't working for me. I wasn't making any real progress in my studies and I was getting discouraged.

My daughter and her family would come over to visit for a weekend. My grandsons were younger at the time and their twin beds were in the room I was using for my office. I had to pick up all my papers, put everything away; I had to take my books and notes and everything I was working on out of that room. After the weekend it would take me about a week to get things back and organized for study. Then my other daughter and her husband would arrive and I'd do this moving out thing again. It was very hard for me to have the focus I needed to do serious work.

Now I have this small office. I leave my apartment at 9 a.m., come down to my private space, and I don't come back until sometime after 5. I've had a work routine since I was in my 20's, and once I'd returned to that rhythm I started doing much better in my studies. It's like going to the office, like going to work. It has made all the difference for me. I spend the majority of my time here alone, and I enjoy the solitude and quiet.

Since finishing my Ph.D. studies and earning my degree, I've been elected to the Alumni Trustee of my University as well as the Alumni Council of my university. These obligations that I've taken on have become very time consuming. There are conferences, phone calls, papers to read, research to follow up on. My university-related work now fills at least half of each day. I think of these new commitments as my retirement job. I love every minute of it.

One of the projects I've taken on that I enjoy most is heading up a research group at the university on creative longevity and wisdom. It's become a huge responsibility and I find it very stimulating and interesting. It allows me to

I spent close to 30 years working in school administration, career counseling and various student services and activities, and this experience has taught me how committed you have to be to living your values to change an institution.

remain involved in the issues of diversity, opportunity, and social justice that I've always been committed to. I can give the university the perspective of a person in their 70's; explore ways to develop curriculum, and bring greater diversity to the faculty. I spent close to 30 years working in school administration, career counseling and various student services and activities, and this experience has taught me how committed you have to be to *living* your values to change an institution.

I'm beginning to see a pattern in how I now choose to spend

my days. I call it, "What am I giving to myself and also giving back to others?" Because the university gave me the opportunity to go back to get my advanced degree, I want to give something to others. I guess these feelings grow out of gratitude for that opportunity. It gave me a new confidence and helped me define a purpose and a new direction in my life. I feel that it's a time in my life to give back to others as well as to myself.

Now in my mid-70's I've finally embraced with a deep confidence what I know and what I believe. Thirty years ago I would have spoken more emotionally; now I can reason better and I've developed the ability to express what matters to me clearly to other people. I sort of metamorphosed into another person – a different me. While I was in the doctoral program my intellectual confidence grew along with a growing appreciation of myself. I really didn't have this in my life before. Even when I was in a position of authority, I didn't feel the authority inside.

I was always outwardly successful but I wasn't able to give myself credit for my accomplishments. People admired me; I always had performed exceedingly well. But in my own mind it seemed I didn't know enough. I just didn't have a marker for self appreciation so all of my accomplishments didn't actually make me any stronger, more self assured, or more confident.

Also as I continue to grow in my later years, I've realized that I never thought of myself as a creative person. I wasn't good at piano as a child. My sister was better. I wasn't good in art classes. It took me a long time to realize that painting pictures and ideas with my mind made me as creative as if I painted a canvas, sang in a choir, or played a musical instrument. I now recognize and fully embrace the originality and creativity I express in my thinking. In the work I'm doing now with the university I'm enormously creative.

This conversation brings to mind something else I want to share. These days we often hear people say things like the mind is connected to the body. I now have experienced that there's a cyclical feedback. I've always been tall and slender but not strong. I have a good deal of lower back fragility and I had the intention to put new strength into my back. About four months ago I decided to work out regularly with a trainer. It hasn't been easy, but the payoff has been remarkable. My body balance is stronger and I have more flexibility. What I can do completely amazes me. I've become an incredibly physically strong person, and although I don't know exactly how to explain this, my body confidence has changed. It's a new kind of discipline for my body, and it's carried into a new kind of discipline for my mind, my body's new strength somehow feeds my mind. This is a wonderful time of my life.

As Allison reflected on her new self-confidence, the ability to accept genuine admiration, and a sense of being in control of her life, she looked back on an earlier time in her life of stress, overwhelm, and confusion.

Her father was very ill with congestive heart failure and couldn't leave the house, and her mother's memory loss indicated early dementia. Every weekend for five years she commuted to their home to provide care.

Those years were a very difficult time for me. I voluntarily took on the responsibility of the primary caregiver. All of my education and work experience wasn't the training or knowledge that was useful when I was dealing with a cardiologist dad who can't breathe well yet thinks he knows it all, and a mom who was by that time living with physical deterioration along with dementia.

I was committed to their care but I was stressed and frustrated. I realized that I badly needed some emotional support.

I didn't hesitate to seek out a therapist. I felt I needed guidance to help me deal with the illnesses and anticipated deaths of my parents. It troubled me that I never had really understood my parents or had been able to come to any resolution of my feelings toward either of them. My mother had always been an emotionally needy person, and my dad, although he began to admire me as an adult, offered little guidance and virtually ignored me when I was young. I remember once asking my dad to tell me some stories about when I was a child. His response was that he could recall stories about my sister but none at all about me. Not everyone needs or wants the kind of introspection that I craved at that time, but I desperately needed it.

It troubled me that I never had really understood my parents or had been able to come to any resolution of my feelings toward either of them.

I sought out an older woman therapist to help me get a better understanding of myself, to look inward and help me grow outward. I don't know where I got the strength to venture down the road of psycho-analysis. I barely had the money to afford it and couldn't get insurance re-imbursement to subsidize it. Yet somehow I was confident that this was the right path for me. I had a strong commitment to resolving my parent issues and get the help I needed to move ahead and keep re-inventing myself. I did some really hard and sometimes painful work in therapy over a long period of time.

I suppose I would have had a good life without the therapy. Yet I have a new richness of understanding that I wouldn't have had without delving into my childhood, getting a deeper perspective on my father and my mother and an understanding of how my young experiences shaped my attitudes on racism. Although there were many times as I grew up that my parents exhibited negative racial attitudes, I never saw things their way. I remember was the first time I became aware of my mother's strong feeling on such things.

I was young, maybe around six years old, a young black woman lived with us and helped my mother with things in the house. Her sister lived on a farm far out of the city and my mother would drive out there once a week to leave our laundry with her sister to be washed and ironed. One time I drove there with my mother. I didn't want to stay in the car so I went into the farmhouse and played with the children. On the way home my mother said, "Never go in that dirty farmhouse again." I didn't understand my mother's demands but I could tell she felt that black people were inferior to us. My father also reinforced that negative attitude, yet even as a child I couldn't embrace that kind of thinking as my own. My therapy brought stories like these to light and for me.

I don't think I would have the joy I have in life at this time without the benefit of so many things I became aware of in therapy. I have new insights into my parents, who they were, who I am, and my separateness from them. I've learned to appreciate and relish quiet and solitude, to read and think and be alone which I truly enjoy. I no longer feel a need to say "yes" to everything. I pick and choose my commitments and I've learned to be comfortable with the decisions I make. I've learned to stay away from some people who are toxic for me and I take deeper pleasure out of the relationships I treasure.

So that's who I am now. But you also asked about who I was. I'll tell you a little more about that so you can get a broader perspective on my life and the changes I've made. When I was raising my daughters it was the best of times, but when they grew up and left I didn't feel bad. It was time for them to go on their own. Both daughters are married and both of them live with their families three or four hours away. I have 3 grandchildren and 2 step-grandchildren. I talk to each daughter once a week and we also keep in touch by e-mail. I have good relationships with both of my daughters but I'm not a constant presence in their lives or with our grandchildren.

> *When I listen to most of my peers who are grandparents, I know that our relationship with the grandchildren is quite different.*

Unlike many grandparents, my husband and I didn't want to be in our grandchildren's daily lives or be baby sitters, so the physical distance we live apart is fine with us. When I listen to most of my peers who are grandparents, I know that our relationship with the grandchildren is quite different. Their children and grandchildren are a constant presence their lives. I know that I wouldn't enjoy that. But we love our grandchildren and we wanted each of them to have occasions of significance to remember. We've done that by traveling with each of them, one at a time so they have a memory of a trip with us just for them. We also have a beach house so they can come and be alone with their grandparents in that setting. We've done that several times and enjoyed each other and gotten to know them in a different way than when their parents are around.

My husband is also in his mid-70's and we've been married for 52 years. I'm not saying that he's an easy person to live with and that we always get along because that isn't true. But I know where to get the juice in the relationship, know the joy, and not get upset at the rest. The emotional boat doesn't rock as much as it used to.

He's a senior judge and he's still working full-time, but he's now taking more time off. He works about four fifths of the year. When he gets assigned a case we never know how long it will take.

I do the food shopping and cleaning and my husband cooks. I've always eaten a more healthy diet than my husband. As we learn more about our bodies, our health and what we eat, he hasn't made any effort to adjust his diet. He's rather cavalier about all of that; he likes cream in his cereal and coffee, and his sweet tooth rules his meal. He also has some genetics that he brings along with him. He has a disposition to heart disease. He carries a lot of risk factors with him. Not long ago his heart went into atrial-fibrillation and he's developed type 2 diabetes, and also an acute bursitis in his right hip, most probably from having childhood polio that left him with one leg shorter than the other. He's going to a post-polio specialist now. All of these things happened in a cluster. He won't talk much about these things with me but I know he's suffering. He operates from a position of denial. That's how he copes with disability.

When we were at the beach this summer, where we used to walk 3-5 miles every day, we didn't walk at all. My husband could barely get around indoors. So our lives have changed a good deal. In my heart and soul and mind I'm a caretaker, a nurturer. So I carry the anxiety for both or us. He can't express it or accept it but I find his physical condition more serious than he seems to view it. He takes a pile of medications. I'm upset about this immediate situation but I also know he could live many years. Yet I do feel vulnerable. I've never lived by myself. I was married right out of college. This new situation in my life is hard for me, and although I need to talk about it, I see that my husband is either unwilling or unable to discuss the reality of his health situation. Yes, I'm crying as I tell you this. It's very challenging coming into this stage of life.

Recently I had a conversation with my husband about aging, about long marriages, and the reality that one of us will die and leave the other. He doesn't want to talk about these kinds of things either. But I often think about what my life might be like as a widow. Yes, I know I said I liked being alone all day but that's because I can look forward to coming home, sitting down with my husband and sharing our day. I very much enjoy a drink and meal together. I'm at a time in my life that I truly appreciate each day we have together and deeply understand and appreciate how much each day matters.

I looked at my watch and realized that our conversation would end soon. Allison looked around the room and smiled softly with a look of peace and contentment on her face. I decided not to ask a specific question but waited for her to speak.

I keep thinking about the idea that I'm in the process of becoming. My life has taken a new turn, a new and stimulating pattern. I've taken on a major commitment with the university for the next three years. I'm looking forward to accomplishing a lot of different things. Meanwhile my current concerns also becoming more mindful, more pro-active about preventive health care. I've given myself permission to take a long walk if I feel I need it. I just leave the dishes in the sink or the letter I'm writing half done and go.

I'm still teaching in the Life Long Learning program at a four-year college. Most of my students are in their 70's and 80's. I call my class Creative Aging. It's a mix of the psychology, attitude, healthy habits, creativity, and continued learning. I do have private clients and I like that more than teaching. I call myself a "Counselor" which I have been since 1975. I've always had a few private clients; I'm really good at that. With older clients the concern might be the transition from work to some kind of partial or full retirement, it may be about being older and not having a positive attitude about embracing the changes that have come with their aging. I also have counseled about sorrow and the grief of losing of persons dear to someone, learning how to be appreciative and kind to oneself for whatever time it takes one to mourn, or to heal, or to adjust.

I've limited the number of the private clients I see. I want to and need to carve out time for myself, my reading, and the things in my life that I see are nourishing me so well. I have a strong interest at this time of my life to continue learning. I try to read everything I can get my hands on related to aging. My pleasure is to write and read and listen to classical music. All of that makes for full and satisfying days. I'd like to take 10 different courses. I'm taking a film class right now. There's a music appreciation class I plan to take. Subjects that I want to study are like a buffet, not of food but of so many good things to do. I've always worked and now I have more leisure to do such things and that's very exciting for me.

> *By spiritual I mean more about taking in the goodness of life, knowing what carries meaning, and what really matters.*

I've always been a spiritual person although I didn't have a name for it. By spiritual I mean more about taking in the goodness of life, knowing what carries meaning, and what really matters. I'm not a religious person but I'm definitely a spiritual person. I've always had an appreciation of each day. Oh yes, I have bad days and I get sad, and I think I was sad a lot of times as a child. When I'm down it takes the joy and the playfulness out of me, takes away my happiness and depletes my energy. At such times I do a simple thing for myself like take a long walk in the park. Just doing that can change my mood and get me outside of my head. I have ways to get past the sadness and depression that I didn't have when I was younger.

I'm now following the guidance I've often given others, to find their way to some internal respite and peace. One day at a time is always a wise philosophy, and indeed I deeply and honestly embrace the essence of each day. It isn't just recently that I've been interested in efforts to live in the moment and stay centered. I've begun to think of myself more as a philosopher of aging than a practitioner. Of course I realize that we all have different life situations and must find our own path to deal with both challenges and opportunities.

When I see what I've accomplished in building body strength, along with my accomplishments in intellectual growth, I can hardly believe it. I took on something to challenge myself, to reach beyond my comfort zone, and that saved me from narrowing myself down into a safe zone as many older people do. I reached for something new; a challenge to expand my life that brought a new and different outlook into it. Although everyone's situation is unique, I'd tell every women in her mid-life years and older to expand her thinking, surprise herself, choose something to do that would challenge her and take her beyond her boundaries, and energize her life. But be selective. I've learned that it's OK to try something, and if it doesn't satisfy, doesn't work for you, then move on and try something else.

I guess I pretty much have said what I have to say except for one thing more; I know one thing for sure—you've got to wake up in the morning with direction, some purpose that will shape your day, something to do. That meaning, that purpose takes charge. It gives you the energy to get through the day. It's very important that I say once more that I'm happier, more content, more pleased with my life than at any time in the pasts. My aging has brought me a wonderful, unexpected opportunity. I look at this time of my life as the very best time of my life.

> *Joy is what happens to us when we allow ourselves*
> *to recognize how good things really are.*
> – Marianne Williamson

AFTERTHOUGHTS

Allison's story got me thinking, once again, about how much energy and courage it takes to let go of old patterns, especially when they're pretty comfortable, in order to see the possibilities for change open up. Allison left her position as the creator and moderator of the minority roundtable for lawyers. Yet she sensed that there were other opportunities for her that could in some manner enrich her perspective and carry on the work she felt strongly about in some new way.

It was easy in retrospect for her to tell her story because earning her advance degree had already put her in a position to support new work in racial and age integration. Yet, even with high hopes, we can't know where such a decision will actually take us. What one older person I met recently termed "fierce determination" seems to be present in many persons in their 60's, 70's, and 80's when a path for change is chosen.

I understand and empathize with Allison's concern and fears over her husband's changing level of activity. Her comments about the walk on the beach that she and her husband could no longer take together is a familiar scenario to me. Recently I collected a series of interviews with family caregivers, and every spouse, life partner, or significant other I talked with described how the pattern of mutually shared activities changed drastically when illness or disability demanded adjustments be made.

I appreciate and admire Allison's statement that she continues to be in the process of becoming. Even in these times when the phrase "positive aging" has become part of our everyday vocabulary, I'm aware that in our later years we often don't believe that the future holds new opportunities. Some of that old myth persists—the idea that older persons don't change, don't learn, don't matter as much as younger people. I challenge you to view those opinions critically.

As you read Allison's story, what thoughts about your own life, your continued growth and adaptability to change, came to mind? Who are you now that you're no longer who you were? Allison's story is a challenge to move closer to our essence as we age. I liken the process to coming closer to our own core.

Eve (age 65)

*As I began to take stock of my life and make new and
different choices, I perceived this period as one of
reflection and discovery during which I was able to look both
backward and forward with a certain measure of experience.*

— Elllen Sue Stern

**I worked with Eve at a conference session entitled, *On Being
An Older Woman*. The workshop attracted women of a
wide range of ages, some in their thirties, others having just
celebrated their eightieth birthday. The session included
a good deal of personal sharing. It was comfortable to be
part of a group of women of such varied stages of life who
openly shared deep feelings, hopes and fears with each other.
I met with Eve after her session and the mood of openness
continued as she talked of her own experiences of becoming
an older woman.**

A year ago I turned 65. I've had a career in the field of geriatric social work and dealt with older persons for many years;
now I was on the cusp of becoming one of them. When I got my
Medicare card it was a shock. I remember saying out loud, "This
can't be mine; this is some mistake!" I realized there was ageism

in my reaction. There have been other moments like that where my response to my own aging reflected a negative or unaccepting attitude. I'm certain that I'm not alone in such reactions; many of us don't readily accept and embrace our own aging. I looked at that birthday as kind of a milestone, an opportunity to spend the year consciously exploring my transition into a new stage of life. Now I'm 66. I'm still spending a good deal of time thinking deeply about my aging process. I have a new honesty with myself. I think of my aging as a partner in my growth at this time of my life.

I grew up in a family where the women were always conceding to the men and I picked up the feeling, I guess, that that's the way you do it. It was that old fashioned thing—the men were more important, and the women just sort of held everything together. My family was very open-minded so it wasn't an oppressive sort of a thing, just an acceptance of traditional roles.

I was married in my 20's, at a time when the Women's Movement was just beginning. There was a new kind of thinking that began slowly to make me aware of things I had never noticed before. For example, at every meeting or group gathering I was at the women were making the coffee and serving the refreshments and then leaving the room. I started thinking that I didn't want to take the meeting notes, bake the cookies, and spend the rest of the time in the kitchen while the men were making decisions. I heard about a consciousness-raising group in the city we were living in, and a friend and I went to some of their meetings. I realized I had grown up in a sexist society that defined women as less than men, a world where the goal of life was to grow up to please men and to be 'the other.' I began to see that there could be other choices and I got very involved with some of the Women's Movement initiatives. And it transformed my life.

I joined a group that felt that if it was our choice, having kids was a wonderful thing. I concentrated on exploring issues around childbirth, choice, and the various reasons that motivate women to decide to have children. I was pregnant at the time and really wanted children. At the time of delivery, I was faced with a challenge because those were times when we enlightened women wanted natural childbirth. We considered having a C-section a compromise. However, at the last minute I decided to have a caesarian section because of necessity. I learned from that experience that a militant attitude without compromise isn't a good stance.

I continued to work with my women's group when I was a mom at home. The subject of child bearing and young women who were mothers was my particular interest at that time. My focus was on whether women were having babies because that was an expected role, or by their own timing and choice. My exploration of cultural expectations of women in the childbearing age and how those expectations affected their personal decisions gave me the opportunity to contribute to a book that became very important to the Women's Movement called *Our Bodies, Ourselves*.

...we enlightened women wanted natural childbirth... However, at the last minute I decided to have a caesarian section because of necessity. I learned from that experience that a militant attitude without compromise isn't a good stance.

We now have two grown sons. When they were young I enjoyed staying home with them full-time for seven years. Then I decided to go back to the university to study for a degree in social work and psychology. My goal was to work with mothers and children and to train myself to serve their young families.

Part of a requirement in one of the courses I was taking was working for a time in a mental health hospital. I rotated in a geriatric unit. I really loved being with older people. Most of the older persons in treatment had good lives in their earlier years but were having problems in later life. Many of the people were suffering from some form of depression. I learned a tremendous amount working with older persons. It just seemed natural for me in many ways because I had grown up in an intergenerational household with grandparents, aunts, and people in all ages and stages of life. When I graduated in the mid-1980's, social work was not an expanding field and funds for many jobs in that area of work were drying up. The only employment I was able to get was a part-time job. It was working with older clients at a community mental health agency.

My work was with older persons but my passion at that time was to my women's group, and our focus on subjects related to the growing Women's Movement. Again I worked with them on a section of another book, *Women Growing Older* and a year later, *Our Bodies, Ourselves—Menopause.* So I was working on the concerns of young women and had a job that kept me interested and involved with the subject of aging. I enjoyed both the work with older persons and my involvement with the Women's Movement. Both ends of the aging spectrum were important concerns of mine but I never wanted either to become a higher priority than my family. I've always been very home centered and never sought a full time career.

I recalled that Eve had talked about art and how important painting had become to her shortly after her 65th birthday.

Both of my parents were teachers and I guess that made me want to have a similar kind of work. When I was younger I tried being an artist for a while but that solitary life—being alone, day after day, trying to make a work of art—just didn't appeal to me. I'm a very gregarious, social kind of person, and I finally gave up painting entirely. That was OK for me then, but as far as teaching went, to give that up wasn't OK. I was able to get involved in an experimental education program for children from kindergarten through grade twelve as well as teacher training programs.

Now I've taken up painting again and I'm really enjoying that. My painting is for my own enjoyment. I don't want to make it a career or my work. I wanted to bring it back into my life, to find what I had enjoyed about painting many years ago and what it meant to me personally. I went to a holistic heath center and took a course they were offering on yoga and watercolors. I thought that would be a great way to get back into art. The instructor in that class put together a book of paintings that were done in our class, and asked us to submit a written piece about the personal meaning of the painting that had been chosen for inclusion. I took that assignment very seriously and wrote a very long piece. I'll share a portion of it with you. After I wrote these words I realized that at this time of my life, my art had once again become a major interest to me.

These paintings are part of a story about my journey as a third age woman reconnecting to a creative process which I had put aside. I went to a watercolor painting retreat in the country feeling that I needed to return to art thru an experience in nature. By breathing deeply, being in the moment, I began to find my authentic way to respond to the visual world with watercolors and I was launched. Since then, painting in the context of this class, I feel an increasingly visual connection to the natural world. The changing seasons, fruit and flowers, the changing landscape, sky, clouds and light are a flow of unique visual moments. I feel I'm in conversation with the paint, the paper and the visual world. Sometimes I respond realistically, sometimes abstractly. This inner urge to paint feels like a more authentic, core response than it did in the early days; I now know that it will sustain me for the rest of my life. Where this will lead I don't know. My perspective has deepened and I'm on an artistic journey that has become part of my sense of vitality and well being.

What I love about watercolor is that it's very spontaneous; things happen on the paper and it's there. You can't go back. It is what it is. There's something very freeing about that for me. I loved the spontaneity of it. It makes sense to me.

I started taking other watercolor courses. We sometimes write poems with the paintings, we sometimes have small shows, and that's very gratifying. I enjoy it enormously. But – do I want to start painting seriously, work at it like a profession, plan for a show, and seek out a gallery? I don't know if I want any of that. For now I'm thankful that I'm back into watercolor painting. It's been very gratifying.

My husband retired recently and I feel I need to adjust some of my life to his. I don't know yet exactly how to plan or move ahead with some of my ideas, plans, and time. His new pace is quite different from mine. He's into Life Long Learning courses; taking classes in literature, humanities, arts, journalism. It seems that every new class that's offered interests him. His activities make great dinner conversation. In his work life in medicine he had been a very time conscientious person, very structured and disciplined. Doctors have to be that way. Now he's loose and unstructured. He does a minimal amount of teaching in the medical school but most of his time is spent going to lectures, seminars, and study groups. He's also taking piano lessons. He's very happy in his pursuits. His is a very different rhythm from mine.

It was almost time for Eve's next session at the conference. I didn't want our conversation to end without her talking about her reflections, decisions and insights arrived at during her 65th year.

I don't know yet exactly how to plan or move ahead with some of my ideas and things that I want to bring to my teaching. One thing I know for sure—I no longer want to teach at the university. I feel I can be more effective teaching about life transitions in a more informal community setting. I'd like to continue doing mid-life education for women. I need to pursue a different direction that will allow me to teach what I know. I still continue doing my many projects. I've been working on several committees and initiatives that have to do with menopause and some projects relating specifically to ageism. I hope I can develop some programs exploring the aging process at community centers, schools and other venues.

I used to feel that I needed an identity, a special title or status label to be part of who I was. That used to be so important but it no longer matters to me.

I used to feel that I needed an identity, a special title or status label to be part of who I was. That used to be so important but it no longer matters to me. I've heard people say that in their 60's, 70's and older they feel a greater authenticity without the need to have a label like social worker, professor, vice president, or whatever. There's always been so much emphasis out there to publish and be recognized, to always be busy and productive, to seek the achievement path, the money path; it's the American work ethic, that I, like so many others, abided by. What's most valuable to me at this stage of my life is exactly what the culture doesn't honor. It's a complete change from having to be someone or be known for something. I want to feel that wherever I am or whatever I choose to do, I'm really me—that I'm authentic.

I'm in an ongoing process to define for myself how to live it, how to shape it, how to prioritize my goals. I realize that I'm in limbo and not a bit uncomfortable about that. The way I approach painting, or any other interests that engage my imagination and curiosity, is totally different now than at any other time of my life. I don't know yet exactly how to plan or move ahead with some of my creative ideas. Like I said earlier, I'm still in limbo and for me that's a good place.

I believe each of us, in our own individual way, could listen to that voice inside and let it speak out more loudly.

What is meaningful for me at this time of my life is the questions I ask myself. For me it's just savoring the preciousness of life and of people, relationships; it's searching within for meaning and exploring a different purpose in my life. I think now so often about the beauty of nature and my responsibility to protect the environment, doing what I can to help make our world humane and caring in whatever ways I can. I believe each of us, in our own individual way, could listen to that voice inside and let it speak out more loudly.

I've had an awakening to my mortality. I'm still dealing with the shock of having reached this time of my life. The realization that I have some unknown time limit on my life became a reality when I turned 65. I keep coming back to my recent thoughts about mortality; a realization that I don't have 30 or 40 years ahead. Yet even if time is shorter, I can't tell myself that I have to figure out some plan for the years ahead by some deadline. It isn't happening that way. I trust that the path of my future journey will evolve.

I guess I want to appreciate and validate more consciously the things that I've found to be of value. There's a deeply spiritual thing going on for me. It's not in the framework of organized religion—that hasn't been an important connection—but it may, or may not, lead to what organized religion can offer. I'm open to what's out there in the world if what is inside of me gravitates in that direction.

Something deep is awakening in me. It's all about waking up to myself. I'm quiet at this time in my life. Not everyone will share my values but I've come to believe it's important for each of us, as we enter into our mature years, to seek inside of ourselves for who we are. That's my challenge to myself in the 66th year of my life. I'm just starting to understand concerns like meaning and balance, but I don't feel the need to formulate a plan for the years ahead. Being in limbo gives me no anxiety. Maybe that's wisdom.

AFTERTHOUGHTS

I wonder how many of us got a twinge of connection, or maybe a bolt of awareness, when Eve talked of productivity and being busier than is in our own best interests. I confess that I'm one of those people. Eve's plan to look honestly at her earlier life with a conscious goal of clarifying her needs and values has my admiration. Many of us realize at some point that the values of our younger years no longer fit who we are now. Although Eve chose her 65th year for that evaluation, it can be at any time in our lives when that small voice inside says something like, "this lifestyle isn't working for me anymore."

A woman in her 40's once told me that the pace of her life and the pressures she put on herself was making her physically ill. Her solution to her anxiety and stress (in addition to saying "no" to some offers of work that came her way) was to sit in a public garden for some length of time each day and observe the beauty and quiet around her. She told me it quieted her mind and helped her realize that she no longer enjoyed or wanted the overwhelming pace of life she had chosen. Getting to know ourselves in a deeper way is available at any age if we open the door to that opportunity. I offer you a few inspiring words of others that validate the path of Eve's journey.

> *The woman who is willing to make the change*
> *must become pregnant with herself, at last.*
>
> *– Ursula Le Guin*

> *Pregnant with ourselves, we begin an internal,*
> *Utterly compelling journey towards rebirth.*
>
> *– Ellen Sue Stern*

> *You need to claim the events in your life to make yourself yours.*
> *When you truly possess all you have been and done, which may*
> *take some time, you are fierce with reality.*
>
> *– Florida Scott Maxwell*

Conversations That Can Make a Difference

I've always had a compelling interest in other people's stories. Listening to or reading the stories of others, we laugh, cry, empathize and sympathize. I've found over and over again that I and others gain insight and wisdom from someone we don't personally know and might never meet. As someone reveals their story we discover things about our feelings, aspirations, priorities and values. We share their courage, determination, new learning and strength. Their experience can enrich and inspire us.

People often ask me where I find such interesting people to interview. I tell them what I'm telling you now—Everyone has a story. Just listen with your mind and your heart and they will share their travails and their triumphs. You too have a story that can inspire and inform others.

I hope some of the eighteen stories in this book have offered you some insight and inspiration, a personal gift in disguise. I've said the following five words many times over the years but they remain true for me and I hope for you.

Facts validate but stories illuminate.

About the Author

Connie Goldman is a former daily and weekend host of National Public Radio's *All Things Considered* and also an NPR arts reporter. Her mission for the past quarter century has been to write, speak, and produce public radio specials about transitions in mid-life and the years beyond. Her focus is on deepening and growing in the second half of life and embracing the changes and challenges that come with the passing years.

She is the author of six books and is a recipient of the Senior of the Year award from the American Society on Aging.

More information about Connie Goldman and her work is available on her website, *www.congoldman.org* and she can be reached via e-mail at *congoldman@aol.com*.

When asked where she lives she often replies, "My mailing address is Hudson, Wisconsin. It's the first exit over the river from Minnesota so I'm close to Minneapolis and St. Paul. No matter where I've lived these many years, Minnesota has always been home in my heart!"